You Can Lead

**Your complete guide
to managing people and teams**

Dr Judith A Chapman

Spineless Wonders
ABN 98156041888
PO Box 220 STRAWBERRY HILLS
New South Wales, Australia, 2012

First published by ES-Press,
an imprint of Spineless Wonders, 2016
www.drjudithchapman.com

© Judith Chapman

Cover design and layout by Bettina Kaiser
Typeset in Scala Sans

Printed and bound by Lightning Source Australia

National Library of Australia Cataloguing-in-Publication entry:

Author: Chapman, Judith A
Title: You can lead: your complete guide to managing people and teams
ISBN: 978-1-925052-26-8 (pbk)
Notes: Endnotes
Edition: 1st

Subjects: Leadership development, team leadership, employee engagement
Dewey: 658.4092

Acknowledgements

Many people have contributed to this book through their encouragement, advice and stories about leadership. They come from a variety of professions and backgrounds, but all helped me to believe that completing this project was both possible and worthwhile.

I would especially like to thank Heather Cobban, Peta Murray, Wendy Holland, Katie McMurray, Emma Read and George Rosier for their ongoing support and insightful comments on the text. Numerous others have encouraged my efforts along the way with their friendly enquiries and genuine desire to see the book in print.

Although I am well versed in the science of leadership, my MBA students and the leaders I have coached over the years have kept me grounded in their realities. Learning about their dilemmas and challenges was the reason I decided to write this book. It was my way of assisting more people to establish themselves as inspiring and effective leaders. Several of my colleagues from academia, especially Anneke Fitzgerald and Stan Glaser, have helped me to shape my ideas as an academic, writer and leadership coach.

My thanks also to Bronwyn Mehan and Bettina Kaiser for assistance with the technical aspects of getting the book into print and onto the internet. They could not have been more generous.

This book was written for tomorrow's inspiring leaders. Alexandra Crogan, Joanne Trezise, Darcy Chapman and Katie Cobban, you are among them.

Contents

Introduction

After many years honing your professional skills and developing your competence, you have been recognised and rewarded with that coveted promotion. Now you are accountable for the work of others. You have become an instant leader. It is an exciting new chapter in your career and you want to shine.

You hit the ground running but after a short time in your new role you realise that leading people is not at all easy and there are so many unexpected calls on your time. You have schedules to organise, staff who want answers, clients to keep happy, budgets to plan and meetings to attend. With demands coming from above and below you feel sandwiched.

But you remain idealistic. You came into the job filled with ideas and do not want to lose your enthusiasm. However, putting your ideas into practice is not as easy as you had thought. Some senior people are very demanding, the organisation is not as flexible as you would like, you have to make resources stretch a long way and there are many policies to get your head around. Most of the people in your team are great but, even so, hardly anyone does exactly what you want just because you ask them to. As you now realise, leadership is a juggling act and some of the balls are not easy to catch.

Where do you go for help? Most people like you are left to sort things out for themselves. Your own manager may be too busy to share their time and only the fortunate few are offered leadership training. That is where this book comes in. It is your complete guide to managing people and teams. It is written to help you as you start out in your first leadership role at work. You will find it practical, easy to read and illustrated with stories and examples.

In fact, this book contains so much relevant information that if you have been a leader for some time and would like to rethink your approach you, too, will find it useful. It will refresh your ideas and reinvigorate your leadership.

A noted feature of the book is that it demystifies the idea that to lead you have to have a special personality or 'look the part'. It explains how anyone can establish their leadership by behaving like a person others choose to follow. There is plenty of advice about connecting with people, building relationships based on trust and influencing others to share your vision and enthusiasm. You will also learn how to manage the stresses and the difficult moments, as well as enjoy the successes with your team.

Another feature of this book is that it highlights the three domains around which effective leaders build their knowledge and capabilities. These are:

- focusing individual and team effort
- energising and motivating the team
- creating a positive social climate.

You will learn what each of these involves and the strategies you can use to begin implementing them right away. In addition, you will find detailed advice about what to prioritise during the first 30 days in your new role. Follow this advice and become a leader who is intent on building a team of people who, like you, are engaged, productive and obtain real satisfaction from their work.

Chapter 1 focuses on how leaders behave every day as they build their credibility. It explodes some of the myths about leadership. The central message is that good leadership is about your behaviour, not your personality or background. Leadership is unique to each person and you can find your own niche in your chosen profession.

Chapter 2 looks at the things effective leaders do to harness and focus the energy of their teams. It introduces the three issues (mentioned above) around which you should aim to develop your knowledge and capabilities. It provides enough information to get you started. You will find more detailed guidelines in Chapters 5, 6 and 7.

Chapter 3 highlights the best way to connect with people and build relationships. It also shows you how to use influence and power to increase the team's capability over time. Less effective styles are described as well. While Chapter 2 explains *what* you should do as a leader, this chapter tells you *how* to do it.

Chapter 4 begins with the characteristics of teams where high performance is sustained over the longer term, and then gives a realistic assessment of the factors that can get in the way. It alerts you to the challenges ahead and provides advice about how you can meet them.

Chapters 5, 6 and 7 provide more detail in relation to each of the three knowledge and capability issues that were introduced in Chapter 2. These chapters explain what you can do, often in step-by-step format, to manage the most critical functions of your leadership role.

Chapter 8 is full of useful ideas to help you develop and grow as a leader. This includes checklists of things to do during the first 30 days in your new role. These ideas are arranged around the three knowledge and capability domains so that you do not miss anything that will help get your leadership off to the best start possible.

You can lead if you know how. That is what this book is for, so read on!

4

Chapter 1
The leader in you

Setting an example is not the main means of influencing others, it is the only means.

Albert Einstein

> *In this chapter ...*
>
> *You will discover that good leadership is founded on how you behave every day to establish your credibility with your team. Some of the myths about what makes a good leader will be exploded, and you will see that people like yourself are capable of finding their leadership niche. If you ever wonder whether you have the right stuff to be a leader, then this chapter will dispel your doubts.*

Leading with credibility

When it comes to succeeding in management, more has been said about leadership than any other topic. With all the homilies and advice, why is it still hard to get it right? And why do many new leaders feel so utterly unprepared when the reality of their situation begins to set in?

If you sometimes feel flustered, clueless or just worn down, you are not alone. As a person new to leadership, there will be many occasions when you wonder why you stepped up in the first place, or wish you were back in your old job. As is often said, it's lonely at the top.

This book was written with you in mind. Think of it as your personal guide to the everyday business of leading others in building a productive workplace. Why is it personal? Because it provides advice that you can follow, regardless of your experience or personality. It focuses on what you do on a daily basis to lead your team, not on who you are, what you look like or the profession you are in. The key message is that your success as a leader comes from the things you do every day to establish your credibility with your team. It is a simple but very powerful message. Read this book and learn to behave like the kind of person others choose to follow.

Why is your everyday behaviour so important? It is because you are very visible to your team and they notice everything you do. As leader, you are a role model. Through your behaviour you send important signals about what is important, acceptable standards of behaviour and performance, how people should treat one another, and much more. Finding the leader in you is all about understanding the impact of your behaviour on others, and guiding your team towards results that make all of you proud. Consider this scenario:

> Margo entered the room and took a seat to one side. She had met her new boss, Anthony, just a few times, and was keen to see how he handled the weekly meeting of team leaders in the large physiotherapy department. This was her first ever job as a team leader – she felt apprehensive, but a little excited, too. When Anthony walked purposefully into the room Margo noticed how the chatter died down immediately and all eyes turned in his direction. First, he extended a warm welcome to Margo and another new colleague before starting in on the main agenda. She was surprised to see OH&S raised early, with discussion given to incident reporting procedures – very different from her previous employment where no one quite knew the proper procedure.

> Attention was now focused on the main item: progress towards implementing the new patient management software in their department. There were some problems with it, apparently. Anthony listened to each manager carefully, gave advice and invited others to help pose solutions. Thirty minutes later, after words of appreciation from Anthony for everyone's hard work, the meeting concluded, the atmosphere upbeat. Margo's earlier concerns were replaced with enthusiasm and a desire to report back to her team on the morning's proceedings.

In Anthony, Margo has a great role model for her own leadership. His leadership works – people take notice, contribute, are energised and want to get on with the job. This includes Margo. She now has an idea of some of the priorities (like OH&S) and has found that the culture is open and supportive. Yet she knows little about Anthony's leadership other than through his behaviour at the meeting. She has seen him in action, and that was enough to establish his credibility in her eyes.

So is Anthony different from other people? Not as much as you might think. Could you be a leader like him? Most likely. It is a matter of finding the leader in you. Many people step away from leadership roles because they lack confidence or do not think they have the capability. They see nothing but a huge gap between themselves and the impressive qualities of good or great leaders they have known. They listen to the hype, and think that leaders have to be 'powerful', 'transformational' or 'inspiring', and conclude that they could never measure up.

The truth is that many leaders do not start out feeling at all confident – typically, that comes later. Most are not household names, nor are they impressive figures on a large stage. Leadership roles are of all kinds and are found across all sections of society. Leaders hold lofty positions as business owners and politicians and less visible roles as supervisors, teachers and police sergeants. But when any leader gets the settings right they use power in a positive way; they make a difference and they do inspire others.

Leadership is unique to each person. Like Anthony, you can develop your credibility as a leader so that others want to be in your team. Anthony acts in accordance with all of the principles of behaviour described in this book. They are principles that you can readily customise to fit with your leadership aspirations, profession and workplace.

What makes a leader?

We need to be very clear about what makes a leader, and what does not. Here are three important questions to explore:

1. Are leaders born with the right stuff?

Let's start with the notion that leaders are born with the right set of personal characteristics, like charisma, confidence or drive. The idea that leaders have a special kind of personality goes back a long way, perhaps thousands of years, and is sometimes referred to as the 'great man' theory. The basic idea is that leaders are different from ordinary people – that they are a superior lot. Along with this is the assumption that all leaders are alike in their personality and style – that there is one type of person who is destined to lead.

A lot of research has gone into this theory – the management science equivalent of the search for the Holy Grail. Over the years researchers tried to identify the fixed physical, intellectual and personality traits that distinguished leaders from non-leaders. The question is now decided and it is a case of the great man – not! Some personal characteristics do show up consistently, but their link with leadership is tenuous. To make matters worse for the theory, just about every leader has a different combination of attributes. Take a moment to think about it – how much did Winston Churchill and Mahatma Gandhi have in common?

Still, it is worth knowing what personal attributes have shown up, however modestly, in a cross-section of leaders. These include high levels of personal drive, the desire to lead, honesty, integrity and self-confidence. Also in the mix are intellectual ability (but not too much!), business knowledge, charisma, creativity, flexibility and personal warmth.

All in all, the 'great man' theory is rather disappointing. It provides a starting point, but does not explain many important things about leadership. It is simply not possible to profile the archetypal leader – leaders come in all shapes and sizes! And most are made, not born that way. Further, there are no surprises in the list of attributes in the paragraph above – you already have some of these, and you can develop them further if you choose to.

In short, there is now strong support for the idea that most leadership qualities are consciously developed and evolved. The notion that some people 'have it' and others do not is more or less quashed. Closer to reality is that many (perhaps most) people have sufficient good qualities needed to lead, and that includes you. With experience and determination there is no reason why you should not find your leadership niche.

2. Is leadership something you acquire?

We expect certain people in society to be good leaders, such as politicians, business figures, people prominent in the community and sporting heroes. Many are, but unfortunately others fail to inspire, or even worse, disappoint by betraying our trust or expectations. So, leadership is acquired to the extent that many roles have leadership responsibility. However, it is one thing to hold a 'position of leadership', but quite another to be regarded by others as a credible leader or role model.

Think of senior people you know (or have known) in your workplace, and how impressive they are (or were) as leaders. Chances are you can identify those who are good managers but so-so leaders, and others who are great leaders (and perhaps good managers as well). All of their positions give them formal authority and power. This is necessary for 'business as usual' but it is not enough to inspire people to be involved, energised or creative. If something extra is missing then no amount of formal authority and power will fill the gap.

So, leadership credibility is not automatic. This is true for the most junior of leadership roles, like captain of a sports team, to the very senior, such as CEO or mayor of a local government district. A person may acquire the position, but they still need to work on developing the leadership. This is easier for some people than for others due to previous experience and know-how, a solid track record, or having a cohesive team to work with. But the fact remains, what the person actually does as they build influence and team relationships governs the quality of their leadership.

3. Is leadership something you earn?

You can acquire a leadership position, but credibility as a leader is something you earn. Leaders are not defined by the roles they fill, but by the way they conduct themselves in the role. This has always been so. The Greek philosopher Aristotle taught privileged boys who were destined for leadership positions. For him, being born into the right family was not enough for a boy to fulfil his purpose. The capacity to lead and be a force for good in Athenian society needed to be developed through study and experience. Moral goodness – what we think of as good character and integrity – was the result of discipline and practice. Aristotle believed that leaders had to earn the trust and respect of their followers – in a civil society it was not theirs for the taking.

In other ancient texts this idea was carried over into the military field. According to Sun Tzu in *The Art of War*[1], military commanders needed the trust and confidence of their troops to reliably implement a plan to overcome an enemy. This came from their everyday demonstration of certain qualities – righteousness, acting humanely, behaving with integrity, being trustworthy and having superior intelligence. Holding a position as commander was not enough in itself.

Another military man, Sir William Slim[2], a successful World War II general, made a similar point. 'Any commander's success comes more from being trusted than from being feared, from leading rather than driving.' Military organisations are among the most hierarchical of all and formal authority and power are very important. If they need leaders to earn their place at the helm, then how much more necessary is it for leaders everywhere to do the same?

The idea that leadership is earned is echoed in the contemporary notion of 'followership'[3]. Leaders are in a social relationship with the people they want to influence. People choose to be followers or not – they make an active choice to opt in or opt out. They might be assigned to a team, but unless they accept the leader in their own minds, they are not followers in the truest sense. Followers and leaders act in partnership – they listen, collaborate and share their learning. This is unlikely when leadership claims are based on formal authority or social position alone. We are irritated by people who seem to lack a good grasp of the situation or who act like petty despots. We do not like to do things just because someone tells us to do them. We want to be convinced that it's worth doing, and that we are doing it in the most suitable way.

To turn your team into true followers you need their confidence, trust and support. These things do not attach automatically to you, they are earned. Accepting your leadership is an act of choice that comes down to your personal credibility as a leader. This exists in the minds and hearts of others. It does not stand alone and you cannot claim it for yourself. If you want others to see you as a leader and not just a manager or supervisor, you have to work at it.

Actions speak loudly

Your behaviour and actions define your quality as a leader. Good intentions, promises and clever ideas mean nothing if your deeds do not match your words, you behave inconsistently, or if there is no follow-through. This may seem harsh, but if your people are not performing as you expect, seek answers in your own behaviour first. Chances are, you will find something to work on.

Try to put yourself in your team's shoes and see yourself as they do. This is not easy. Understand that people know you from what you do, not what you think and feel. They cannot see your good intentions, desire to make things better or the reasons why you acted in an apparently inconsistent way. It's your behaviour that is on show, and as the leader you are in a goldfish bowl.

Consider this scenario:

> *Eager to establish his position as a team leader in the Planning Department, Carl stepped into his office 20 minutes before anyone else. It gave him time to get the day organised before the phones started to ring. At drinks with his boss the previous evening Carl learned that an important deadline had been brought forward, and he would need to allocate a team member who would get cracking immediately. He thought of Jon, with whom he had spent some time recently on the company's touch football team – a reliable guy who could take a catch. Usually with a plum project*

like this he would ask around the team to see who was interested, but this time there simply wasn't time. He picked up his phone and made the call to Jon. Later that day he noticed the odd silences as he moved around the floor. Could this be about his decision to put Jon on the project? Really? Didn't people realise that sometimes you just had to make a decision, and they just needed to get on with their jobs?

Carl made the erroneous assumption that the team could see the need for decisive action on his part, and that he was only interested in ensuring that the new deadline was met. In fact, all they saw was his action in sidestepping the usual process and appointing Jon. They knew about the late-night drinks and the football. To them, it was looking like cronyism. Misunderstandings like this happen very easily and quickly, but the ill-feeling they create can last a long time. Leaders need to understand that they are very visible. Inconsistencies in behaviour cause confusion, misunderstandings and an erosion of trust.

When it comes to team members, leaders like to think that they are doing the observing. In fact, most of the observing is the other way around – the boss's behaviour is scrutinised daily for signs of shifting priorities, more or less pressure to perform, tighter timelines, mood changes, unpleasant surprises, where the wind is blowing and the like. How much time do you spend observing your own boss and others senior to you? Quite a lot – and for the same reasons your team observes you. Regardless of what you think of them, a boss plays a big part in our daily work life and career prospects. It pays to know their strengths and weaknesses, likes and dislikes.

Like Carl, one of your most pressing challenges is to become more aware of your own behaviour, observing your own patterns and noticing how your verbal and non-verbal messages are received by others. Some of the key behaviours for you to work on are:

- ✓ listening attentively and with interest to others
- ✓ using body language that fits with what you say
- ✓ explaining the reasons for your actions and decisions
- ✓ practising what you preach

✓ following through on promises made

✓ being a good role model for standards you want from others.

What you do, not who you are

When describing leaders, we often refer to personality characteristics that we think make them stand out from the crowd. But referring to personality is a trap when it comes to describing leaders. It draws our attention away from their everyday action, and the things they do to build their credibility. It can also lead us into confidence-sapping comparisons when we think they have characteristics that we lack and will never have. So remember – your leadership is defined by what you do, not who you are. It is all about your behaviour, and not your personality.

Remember Anthony from our opening scenario? You might describe him as confident, a good communicator and inspiring. You might assume that he was always like this. But it is just as likely that Anthony started out very differently, like anybody else, and developed an admirable behavioural repertoire over time.

Take a moment and ask why people might refer to Anthony as confident and inspiring – look at the behaviour behind the personality. Anthony is 'confident' because he takes charge of the meeting, has a clear agenda and does not need to dominate. He is 'inspiring' because he signals what is important, focuses on finding solutions and leaves people feeling energised and enthusiastic. It is his behaviour that makes the impression.

We could choose just about any personality characteristic and describe the behaviour that goes with it. Someone might be labelled 'arrogant' because they don't listen, refuse advice or constantly talk over others. What of 'integrity'? We have a good sense of what it is, but how do we know when someone has it? From their behaviour, of course. It is a judgement we make based on what we observe. A person has integrity because they behave ethically, consistently and predictably. If their choices are questionable, there is a disconnect between their words and actions, or if they seem to go where the wind is blowing, then we describe them as lacking in integrity. It therefore makes sense to see integrity as a set of behaviours – a person acting with integrity – rather than a fixed personality attribute.

Developing trust in a leader is also about our observations of their behaviour over a period of time. When trust is present we are confident that they will treat us fairly, look after our interests at work and deliver on promises. As Stephen Covey[4] said: 'If you want to be trusted, be trustworthy.'

Perhaps you now see that personality characteristics are just descriptions of the behaviour patterns on show. The message here is that you, too, can be like Anthony – confident, a good communicator and inspiring. There is no need for you to worry about whether or not you have the right personality – simply mould your own behaviour so that others see you as such.

Many leaders have doubts about their capacity to lead at some point in their career, but find the resources within themselves to succeed. Gail Kelly[5] is one person who did just that.

Gail Kelly – profile of a leader

In 2008 Gail Kelly was appointed CEO of Westpac, one of Australia's leading financial businesses, and led this institution successfully until her retirement in 2015. Every year from 2010 she was listed by Forbes as among the most powerful women in the world and in 2014 topped the list of powerful Asia-Pacific women.

For a senior banker, her career path was unusual. Kelly was born in Pretoria, South Africa, and completed an Arts degree and Diploma in Education at the University of Cape Town. She taught at schools in Zimbabwe and South Africa for a few years before reconsidering her career choice. In 1980 she joined Nedcor Bank as a teller and ten years later, after completing an MBA and being fast-tracked for her obvious talent, became head of human resources.

With her family she moved to Australia in 1997 and was appointed to the position of General Manager of Strategic Marketing in the Commonwealth Bank. Later, she was put in charge of the bank's large branch network. In 2002 Kelly became the CEO of the struggling St. George Bank and made it a much more profitable enterprise. Shortly after becoming CEO of Westpac, she led a successful takeover of St. George.

Kelly gave strong weight to gathering the best people she could find around her and creating an environment where they could do their best work. She enjoyed being with a team that liked working together and was focused on achievement. She chose people who were engaged, positive, willing and energetic, and avoided those who were arrogant or self-serving.

Kelly freely admitted that on several occasions she had to confront fears that she was not good enough or lacked the skills and experience needed for a senior role. One of these times was when she was offered the human resources lead at Nedcor. She had to pause, dig deep and find the courage to give it a go. Had she not done so, her career would have been very different.

Kelly's advice to up-and-coming leaders is to choose to respond positively to situations and opportunities, be courageous when they do come your way, work with people who energise you, and learn to communicate in a crystal clear way the vision and purpose of your organisation.

Who do you strive to be as a leader?

While your everyday behaviour is important for your credibility, as a leader you will benefit from having a set of values or guiding principles that give direction to your leadership. You might call it a leadership philosophy or purpose. It could be about the kind of leader you want to be, the difference you want to make, or the positive influence you want to have on the people in your team.

Everyone has a leadership philosophy, whether they are aware of it, or not. If we asked Anthony, who holds a senior position in a large hospital, he might say that he strives to build a centre of excellence where cohesive teams deliver the best possible outcomes for patients. You can see how this comes out in his behaviour at the team meeting, and the impact on Margo and others who were present. He is inclusive, inviting input and encouraging people to work together. We can surmise that he is very good at putting his leadership philosophy into action.

You may be curious as to the leadership philosophy of other leaders like yourself. The statements below were provided especially for this book by several leaders when asked: 'Who do you strive to be as a leader?' Take a few moments to consider your own response to this question. Write it down and return to it often as you read this book. You should aim to build a philosophy that is as inspiring as these are.

Who do I strive to be as a leader?

I strive to be my 'ideal' self, that person between who I am and what others believe I need to be. ~ James Hondros

I strive to remain authentic, to be of service to my team without losing myself; to remain useful and purposeful and lead through whatever the system we are part of is doing, planning and striving for. ~ Jen Rossiters

I strive to build the capability in others to be the best they can be and really shine, so that the team can deliver amazing outcomes they never thought possible. ~ Margaret Wright

I strive to illustrate the value that each employee adds, to have clear expectations of performance and to dish out recognition. ~ Ian Pratt

I strive to earn respect by making commitments and sticking by them; I encourage people to make their own decisions and stand by them regardless of results. ~ Kourosh Keshavarz

In leadership, as in life, I strive to treat people as I would like to be treated in that situation, making sure every decision aligns with my core values, such as respect. ~ Belinda Wheatley

I strive to be the person that I know my children will look up to, feel proud to be part of and boast about to their friends – patient, smart, committed and a listener. ~ Jane Toohey

Starting small and building up

It can take time for a newly formed team to perform at its best, and this goes for an established team with a new leader. People need to get to know their new leader's style, adjust to some different expectations and re-establish or surpass previous levels of trust and collaboration.

You were chosen for the leadership role for good reasons. It might have been because of your high level of knowledge or expertise, your organisational skills, your capacity to think strategically or a combination of all three. Any of these should get you off to a good start, but you will need to keep building. There might be pockets of resistance for any number of reasons. For instance, past leaders may have had a very different approach from yours. You might be the first woman to lead in a male-dominated profession, or be from a different cultural group. Morale in your team might be at an all-time low. The list could go on.

There is a first time for every leader. You will know of many impressive leaders who started small or with very little support, people like Mother Teresa and Nelson Mandela. In the beginning, their circle of influence and credibility was limited. But on the other hand, each had a strong sense that something needed to be done and they persevered. You might say these leaders espoused a powerful vision. Over time, through their words and actions they came to represent something of great importance to other people. Ultimately, they developed the capacity to inspire many.

You might wonder if there are any comparisons to be made between leaders such as these, and yourself or others like you. Yes, of course there are. You, too, will need to persevere and build gradually. You, too, will benefit from having a 'vision' for your leadership role, a higher purpose that keeps you going. Thinking about who you strive to be as a leader is a good place to start.

Over to you

Having read this chapter you should be much more confident in your own capacity to lead. If you started out by thinking that you lack the charisma, personal magnetism or drive, then you should now realise that leaders are of all kinds. They are not cut from the same cloth, and personality is just a small part of the equation.

To become an effective leader you need to work on establishing your credibility with your team. A great place to start is by reflecting on your current behaviour. Notice your own patterns, how you typically respond in different situations, and how others react to you. Build on the things that energise and include people. In addition, think carefully about who you strive to be as a leader, and work on ways to make it a reality.

The message is clear. How you behave every day – what is on show to your team – counts above all else. It's about what you do and who you become. You don't have to be a 'great man', but it is important to behave consistently, and to have a leadership philosophy to guide you. The remaining chapters of this book will provide all the information necessary to find the leader in you.

Chapter 2
Your leadership in action

'How do you know I'm mad?' said Alice.
'You must be,' said the Cat,
'or you wouldn't have come here.'

In this chapter ...

You will read about the typical challenges faced by new leaders like yourself. You will also discover how effective leaders add value in their organisations and what you can do to develop a well-rounded approach to your leadership role. By the close of the chapter you will be aware of the three areas where you should aim to build your knowledge and capabilities to fully establish yourself as a leader.

Stepping into the leadership role

In the first days and weeks after you step into your new role you will discover that life at work will never be the same. Here are three challenges that will come out to meet you from day 1:

- prioritising leadership as a time commitment
- leaving the technical/operational comfort zone
- transitioning from colleague to manager/leader.

It can come as quite a shock to discover that being a leader is rather time consuming. So much extra paperwork, countless meetings and those endless requests for your time! However, experienced leaders will tell you that the time you put into familiarising yourself with your new role pays dividends. It would be a mistake to try fitting leadership in around your old role while continuing on as before. You accepted the job and now it is time to step up.

Are you a good organiser by nature, or do you tend to bounce from one project to another, finishing some, and promising yourself that you will get back to the others at some time or another? You will need to develop organisational skills, firstly to manage yourself so that you can fit everything in and, secondly, because organising the work of other people is part of the job.

If you can, compartmentalise your time to some degree, making it clear when your door is open, and just as importantly, when you need time by yourself to do the thinking. Expect to be interrupted sometimes because emergencies tend to have a low threshold – for some people the day is full of matters that need to be fixed now. Get into good habits around reading and responding to emails and other communications. Take time out for lunch and go outside for a ten-minute walk when the stress is building – it will make a real difference.

It is not necessary for you to know more, or to be a better practitioner than anyone else in your team. Many people are very effective leaders in situations where they have less professional knowledge than others around them – but are very good at developing and harnessing the expertise that others have to offer. The better they become at doing their jobs, the more it reflects well on you.

What really counts is the way you use your expertise. If you are like most others in your situation, you have a great deal of it. In fact, this is probably one of the main reasons why you were promoted. But as the leader, it is no longer just about what you can do professionally, but how you use your expertise to make sound judgements that affect the whole team, your ability to build the support of those more senior to you, and your capacity to organise the overall team effort to get the best results.

You might sometimes be tempted to slip back into your former role as a completer of projects, rather than sticking to your current role as leader and organiser. It is a safe haven that gave you a lot of satisfaction in the past. Now it is someone else's job. If you are unable to let go and allow your former close colleagues do the work three things can happen. First, you will reduce their elbow room and give the impression that they aren't up to the job or that you think you can do it better. Result? Loss of motivation. Second, the other team members (if there are others with whom you did not work as closely in the past) will resent the fact that you are spending most of your time with your old group. Result? Feelings of inequity resulting in loss of motivation. Third, you will neglect your real job, which is attending to strategy and organising the overall effort. Result? Loss of focus and attention to the bigger picture.

Of course, you should be in there encouraging and coaching the team. But there is a difference between helping someone with less experience and taking over. As soon as they can do it independently, back off. Check in with them on a regular basis, but it is just as important that they are confident in approaching you for assistance when they need it.

Now this is probably the biggest shock of all – as a leader your relationships with people who were previously friends and colleagues at the same level will necessarily evolve into something different. You used to discuss company policies and your boss quite freely. You cannot do that anymore. Try to cultivate a degree of professional distance with regard to work matters, for example, by ceasing to discuss your feelings about people and company policies in the way that you used to. If you can do this much, you will generally find that genuine friendships continue. Indeed, your old colleagues will also be seeking ways to transition the relationship so that they do not lose a friendship they also value.

A note on your legal obligations

People who are new to the team leader role are rarely briefed about the statutory responsibilities that go with their position. We do not often use the term 'legal-rational authority[6]' when referring to a management role, but strictly speaking, that is what you have. Under the laws of many countries, when you are appointed by your organisation to a management role, you take on certain legal obligations. That also means you can be held accountable if you do not carry them through.

Can you list the legal obligations that you signed up to when you accepted your position? They would almost certainly include equity in employment practices and responsibility for occupational health and safety. In the case of the latter, you are required to maintain a work environment that is free of hazards causing illness or accidents. In Australia, any WorkCover investigation after a reportable incident will include scrutiny of your role in it and any oversight on your part. Hazards are defined broadly and can include anything from exposure to harmful chemicals to a culture of bullying. So if you are not sure, check with your human resources adviser and inform yourself of your obligations.

What are leaders for?

Simply put, leaders are for shaping the action. Their role is to get things done by harnessing the energy that others have to offer. Fundamentally, their job is to help people focus on tasks and outputs, to do things to the required standard, and to get them done within certain parameters. But nothing stays the same for long so the best leaders also inspire teamwork, learning, creativity and a desire to grow and change. To shape the action in today's world, leaders need the capability to operate on both levels.

Leaders new to the role often assume that once they have explained what needs to be done, the team will just get on with it. But it might not happen like this, even when they are quite capable of doing what is asked. The following scenario expresses the frustration felt by Frank, new manager of the 'fresh and frozen' food department in a suburban supermarket.

How many times had he told them not to stack the packages above the clearly marked line in the frozen food containers? Why did they continue to handle the fresh food without using the gloves required by the health authorities? How difficult could it be to follow simple instructions? He had reminded them often enough.

Frank thought back to his meeting with the store manager, Kaitlin, shortly after he started in the job. She was keen to lift standards after an adverse report by the company's inspection team. With his Diploma in Food Storage and Handling, Frank left the meeting confident that he could make a difference in quick time. He had observed the team closely and identified many errors that the previous manager had tolerated. Over the next three weeks he worked alongside the team, explaining what should be done, demonstrating technique, correcting mistakes and repeating the lessons.

What had changed? Not enough. There was some improvement, especially when he was close by, but it was impossible to watch them all the time. He had even overheard two of the staff saying that the old ways of doing things were just as good, and not such a waste of time. Frank was over it!

All Frank wanted was for people to do what he wanted them to do. In this desire he is not alone. Many team leaders feel the same way, and you might be one of them. The fact is that in most modern workplaces you cannot force people to do anything, or to do it in any particular way. If you have to apply too much pressure or resort to threats you have already lost. Even when asked, people want to feel that they are acting on their own volition, that they have made a choice. It may not be the thing that they would prefer to do, but they see the sense in it and are happy enough to comply.

Of course, good leaders aim for more than compliance. They want willing followers, people who will use their initiative and creativity, and work with them to continually improve. Even small adjustments to routine processes happen more surely and smoothly when the team is both willing and capable. It is easy to underestimate the importance of getting people's buy-in when any change, small or large, is needed.

In the scenario, Frank had the senior position, as well as the expertise from his Diploma in Food Storage and Handling. You might think this should have given him enough authority to shape the action in the way that he wanted to. He did not want much, just for his team to make some changes to their work processes and do it his way. But clearly, something was missing – his credibility with the team. If he had it, they would have been more willing to listen. But as it stands they were simply not ready to work with him to implement better food handling procedures.

What could Frank have done differently? Well, he could have spent time building his relationship with the team, seeing things from their perspective, fostering a more collaborative or consultative climate and gaining their trust and confidence. He might have been too didactic in pointing out errors and demanding that procedures be followed, so perhaps more of a coaching style would have worked better.

What effective leaders do

As a leader, harnessing and focusing the energy of your team to achieve results is your reason for being. Effective leaders do this in two ways. They make sure that team goals are always in sight by clarifying everyone's role and expected contribution, and streamlining team work processes so that they are in line with desired outcomes. They also build a team of people willing to work together to solve problems, find solutions and deliver. As the leader you need to focus on both, treating them as complementary processes.

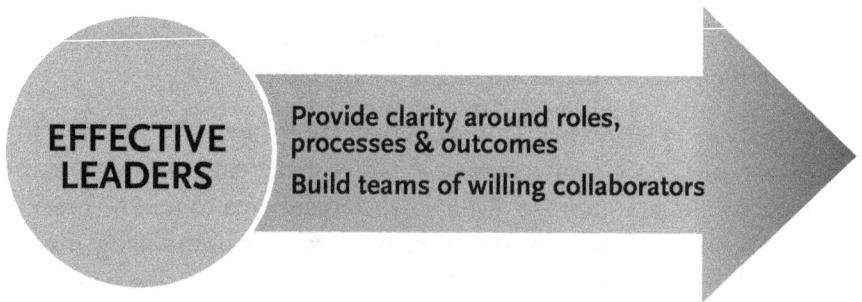

EFFECTIVE LEADERS

Provide clarity around roles, processes & outcomes

Build teams of willing collaborators

As a new leader, it is important for you to make an early start and provide your team with a degree of certainty about your expectations and approach. You want them to be as confident as you are that what you will do together is both achievable and worthwhile. So right now, you want to know what you can do in a practical way to be effective in your role.

The answer lies in three knowledge and capability domains, which are to:

- focus individual and team effort
- energise and motivate the team
- create a positive social climate.

Together, these three domains are central to your role, what you should do to mould your team into a top-performing group of people who produce sustainable results and obtain real satisfaction from their achievements. In the sections below you will find a short introduction to each behaviour set. Then, in Chapters 5, 6 and 7, there will be more detailed, practical ideas that you can start implementing right away.

Focus individual and team effort

When focusing the efforts of your team, here are some key leader behaviours:

- ✓ focusing everyone's effort on tasks linked to company strategy
- ✓ being a great role model for the standards you want others to follow
- ✓ communicating frequently with each person to ensure that their role is clear and unambiguous
- ✓ not blaming people for mistakes – using a coaching style so they are happy to ask when they are unsure
- ✓ being aware of how work flows around your team
- ✓ coordinating work so that it flows smoothly among team members
- ✓ helping poor performers to get back on track.

As leader, one of your most important tasks is to ensure that your team is adding value by delivering results that fit with broader organisational plans and objectives. Start by ensuring that each person in the team is clear about his or her role and responsibilities. Do not assume anything. Lack of role clarity, confusion about the priorities, uncertainty over who is accountable for what and misunderstandings about processes that need to be followed are common in workplaces.

In the following scenario, Frank has arrived at the supermarket well before opening time. He wants to make sure that people on the early morning shift have restocked the produce correctly. He is about to be disappointed.

> Frank strode up to the fruit and vegetable shelves where the produce needing a cool environment was displayed. He noted with disgust that the strawberries were already out, ahead of the more robust fruit with a longer shelf life. Even worse, the shelves were barely below room temperature. He called Jill over as she rushed by, arms laden with bags of oranges.
>
> 'What is going on?' he demanded. 'The refrigeration has only just been turned on. Don't you realise that is the first thing you should do when you come in each morning? And the strawberries and other fragile fruit – you are supposed to bring it out last, after the apples and other stuff that doesn't spoil easily!'
>
> 'Sorry,' replied Jill, stopping in her tracks. 'There is so much to do, I just didn't think about it. I bring stuff out of the storeroom in the order it is packed in the night before and the strawberries were at the front. It's more efficient that way.' Frank walked off in exasperation, mumbling to himself over her lack of common sense.

The point is, common sense is just one person's perspective on an issue that might be much more complex than it appears to be on the surface. As leader, it is best to make sure that everyone understands not only what is expected, but why.

Good leaders hold informal conversations on a regular basis with team members about their roles, achievements and hopes for the future. Apart from being good leadership practice, it helps to prevent the kind of problem that Frank uncovered on his early morning visit to the supermarket.

Most organisations of any size have formal performance appraisal systems to manage individual performance and capability development. No system for performance management is perfect, but if you follow the suggestions in Chapter 5, you and your team should obtain real benefits from both the formal and everyday discussions you hold with them. If your organisation does not have a formal performance appraisal system, consider introducing a process of regular discussions anyway. People crave feedback but many leaders are rather niggardly in giving it.

Also in Chapter 5 you will find plenty of advice on how to improve the performance of a person who is not measuring up. You might be fortunate enough to have a team of top operators, but most leaders have to deal with the problem of an underachiever sooner or later. A typical reaction is to bury your head in the sand, or hope that the person gets the message and lifts their game. The truth is that poor performers rarely change for the better unless they have the support and coaching of a concerned and effective leader.

When it comes to the whole team, you need to consider how the work flows between team members and across to other teams. Do people work intensively together, as they would if they were a team of medical professionals in an operating theatre? Does work flow around the team, with each person adding something, as they would if they were making a piece of furniture, starting with the frame and ending with the fabric covering? Or does each person operate fairly independently, as they would if they were account managers each with their own sales territory?

This issue is important because there are implications for how closely you coordinate everyone's work. If people work fairly independently of one another then close coordination is less of an issue. But if each person relies heavily on one or more of the other team members, then you need to ensure that things are flowing smoothly. You do not want the work to be disrupted by bottlenecks, oversights or conflicts over who is meant to be doing what.

Of course, in focusing the efforts of your team, one factor is overarching – your leadership. The other things you do are important, but they lose their impact when you fail to take an active leadership role.

Through your behaviour you set the standards for others to follow. The performance culture of a team is influenced by the leader more than anything else. The leader models the behaviours they want and expect, and over time this becomes *the way we do things around here*. If people see you do something, they will assume it is okay for them to do the same thing. It might be as simple as the office dress code – dress down and before long people come into work looking too casual. So if you want certain standards to be the norm then you need to live up to them yourself. Be clear that this is about what you do every day. It is not a one-off, and it is not over once you have made an announcement or sent an email around. Generally, people don't listen very hard at meetings, rarely read the policies and procedures manuals, and give only cursory attention to emailed instructions.

So to embed new ideas or ways of doing things, you have to follow through yourself and show people by your example what it means in practice. If you want your team to handle customer enquiries in a certain way, pay attention to technical details, regularly update client files, and so on, then you need to show the way. Your example is the clearest guide others have about what counts and what doesn't. Bypass rules and guidelines, procrastinate over training requests, cancel team meetings without explanation and you are signalling that these things don't matter. Return customer calls promptly, fix things that need to be fixed, follow up on requests, and you are signalling that these things are important.

So leadership is not just in what you say, but also what you do. As a leader you are very visible. Your actions are scrutinised constantly for signs of what matters and what doesn't, and the standards of behaviour and performance that are expected of everyone. Your example is the best tool you have for signalling what the priorities are, and any sense of urgency (or otherwise) about actioning them. Get it right and your team's focus will be where you want it to be.

Energise and motivate the team

Actions you can take to energise and motivate the team include these:

✓ understanding the needs, hopes and aspirations of team members

✓ creating opportunities for people to satisfy their important needs through their efforts and achievements

✓ providing encouragement, coaching and feedback

✓ building positive team relationships and sound communication

- ✓ ensuring that every job contains sufficient interest and challenge
- ✓ linking team members with growth opportunities
- ✓ building a team of people who are purpose-driven.

Galvanising the efforts of everyone in your team brings your leadership to life. It is about creating interest, enthusiasm and a feeling that what you do together is worthwhile. As a person new to leadership, one of your main aspirations is for a team of energised and motivated people who enjoy their work and want to be part of what you are building. Most likely, this is a key aspect of who you strive to be as a leader.

You can build a team like this. It is a matter of understanding some important points about human motivation, and having a plan to put them into practice. In this introductory section we will consider the factors that cause people to put in their best effort or work to their potential, both as individuals and members of a team. Later, in Chapter 6, there will be plenty of advice to help you make it happen.

Let's start with the idea of being energised and active. Here is the key point – people become energised when they have a need or desire that is not satisfied. Some are very basic, like the need to eat and breathe. When you are hungry, for example, you become restless and start looking around for things to eat. Other needs are more complex. For instance, you get an ordinary grade in an exam and are determined to put in more work so you can do better next time. In short, an unsatisfied need stirs you into action. If all goes well the need is satisfied, at least for a time. You can see the way it works from the diagram.

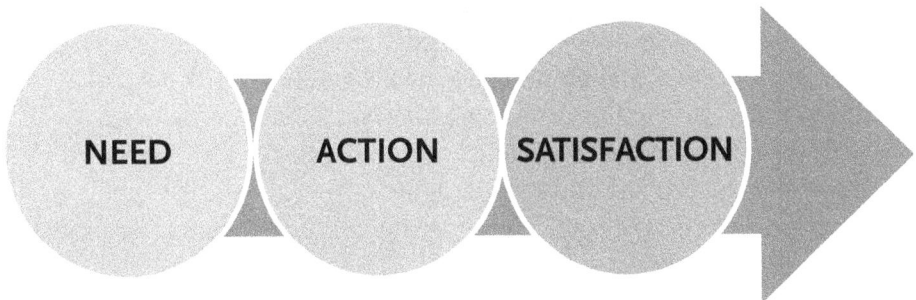

NEED   ACTION   SATISFACTION

So, our behaviour is largely driven by a desire to satisfy our needs. People bring many of their needs to work, including desires to develop their skills, make new friends, earn enough money to pay the mortgage and build a career. If you think about the reasons why you chose your current employer, you will recall that the likelihood of satisfying your important needs was uppermost in your mind. You might have been attracted by the salary, the interesting work, or the chance to lead a team. Perhaps you had two good offers and had to weigh up the merits of each.

You want your workplace to be rich in opportunities for good team members to satisfy their needs, too. For this to happen there have to be clear pathways for people to follow – those that link their work behaviours with the great feeling of having their needs satisfied. They might, for example, be in your team because of the opportunities to learn, or to do work that they believe is worthwhile. This is where your leadership comes in. If you can link the satisfaction of needs like these to work activities, then the team will be focused and motivated to perform.

The idea of a clear pathway between work behaviour and need satisfaction is an important one. People are not robots or circus-trained animals. They think things through, assess the situation and make independent decisions. They watch to see if you follow through on the promises you make, implied or otherwise. You will be sized up for your credibility, influence, consistency and fairness. If you deliver, expect to be greeted each day with a team of energised and enthusiastic people. If you disappoint or let people down, motivation levels will suffer.

Another issue that affects work performance is people's willingness to 'have a go'. Even when the pathway to need satisfaction seems clear from your perspective, some people will hold back. This will happen if they lack self-confidence or feel they do not have the necessary skills, they have failed at similar tasks in the past, or are simply new and inexperienced. As a concerned and supportive leader, your role is to support them with encouragement, coaching and mentoring. In fact, your regular support and feedback on how well the team is progressing towards targets or goals is motivating for everyone.

Let's consider the array of needs that people have. One useful classification is known as Alderfer's ERG theory[7], with three need groups:

Existence: Basic physiological, material and safety needs, including the need for food, housing and an environment free from threats or hazards.

Relatedness: The need to associate with others and to have meaningful relationships, as well as the need to feel the self-esteem that comes from being recognised for our efforts and achievements.

Growth: The need to grow and develop our talent and potential, to be self-directing, to feel good about ourselves (internal self-esteem), and to feel we are connected to a worthwhile or higher purpose.

While we all have many needs in common, each person has a set that is particular to themselves, with different emphases and need strengths. For instance, some people are more interested in money or advancement to a senior position than others. And some of our needs are more or less active at different times in our lives. That is why, as leader, you need to take an interest in each team member, and be aware of the needs uppermost for them at present, as well as their hopes and aspirations.

Everyone has needs in each of the three ERG categories, but is each category equal for motivating them at work? The short answer is 'no'. In general, jobs that provide for existence needs and little else give us a good enough reason to come into work, but to be truly motivating, jobs must satisfy our needs for relatedness and growth. So, work has to be interesting, challenging and have a compelling purpose that fits with our values. It is even better when the whole team shares the same desire to make a difference and can celebrate their achievements with one another.

The point about the importance of growth needs is illustrated in this conversation between Margo, and her boss, Anthony, whom you have already met. Margo, who is new to this hospital, was recently appointed as a team leader in the physiotherapy department. She has met with Anthony to discuss her concerns about low staff morale.

'I'm not sure if I am doing something wrong, but they say it has been like this for some time. Apparently the budget for equipment, overtime and staff training has fallen steadily over the years and it's wearing people down.'

Anthony listened thoughtfully, then asked, 'Who makes up your largest group of patients?'

Margo replied, 'Young children with serious chest infections. We clear the congestion so that the medical staff can treat the underlying condition.'

Anthony asked, 'What could be more important than the work you do with those kids? Has your team lost sight of that?'

Margo considered for a while before saying, 'Maybe they have. But if I remind them, they will feel even worse. There is a new piece of equipment, together with a treatment protocol, that gets better outcomes with the more serious cases but there is no money in the budget to buy it. The physios want to do more for those kids but feel hamstrung.'

'Let me think about it,' said Anthony. 'If I can talk admin into giving us the funding, can you draw the physios' attention to the difference they are making? And undertaking the special training required will give them a boost, too.'

Hopefully, Margo will work with Anthony to lift the sights of her team and energise them with some well-placed reminders about their shared purpose. We will catch up with her in later chapters and see how she is progressing.

Create a positive social climate

Here are some things you can do to create a positive social climate:

- ✓ Be friendly and approachable.
- ✓ Ensure the physical environment at work is pleasant and conducive to positive team interactions.
- ✓ Encourage team members to treat each other with civility and respect.
- ✓ Treat people fairly and equitably regardless of personal feelings.

✓ Provide opportunities for people to balance their work and other interests and commitments.

✓ Remain calm and predictable in your dealings with others.

The social climate of workplaces has changed radically over the decades. Formality and distance have been replaced by an atmosphere of collegiality and a more personalised connection between employees and their managers. People expect to be listened to by a leader who understands their many needs, including their desire for flexible work arrangements that fit with their complex and busy lives.

As leader, you set the emotional tone of the work environment, and you want it to feel trusting and supportive. An enriched social environment is the foundation for productive work relationships, high-level achievements and individual wellbeing[8]. It is absolutely essential for promoting employee engagement. After all, helping one another to succeed and celebrating milestones as a team go to the heart of who we are as social beings.

A good social climate is based on trust. Here is what Warren Bennis[9], a pioneer in the leadership field, who maintained that above all leaders needed to be authentic, had to say about trust:

✓ Trust binds leaders and followers together.

✓ Trust is the emotional glue of all institutions.

✓ Trust is earned, it is interactive.

✓ Eventually you will be trusted if your actions are the same as your words.

✓ An ingredient of trust is really caring about the fate of others and being on their side.

✓ Leaders who are trusted are consistent and competent.

People do their best work when they feel their important needs are being met and that they can trust and rely on the people around them. Generally speaking, they make better decisions, work more collaboratively and are more creative than they are likely to be where the social climate is less pleasant or even corrosive. Factors that reduce the quality of the social climate include criticism, lack of civility, bullying and being ignored. When people feel threatened, left on their own or unsure of what to expect when they come into work, their performance suffers. They tend to disengage, lose their motivation, do less and feel more stressed than would otherwise be the case.

An important aspect of your role is to monitor the social climate to ensure that relationships are as they should be. As in most things, lead from the front. Through your everyday behaviour show the team how you expect them to treat one another by being respectful and supportive. Be self-aware and notice the things you do that make people feel included and appreciated. Take note of any of your actions that cause people to draw away from you or the team, or retreat into themselves. These are signs that the social climate is lacking something.

Here is another story about Carl, whom you met in the previous chapter. We pick up the action the day after he bypassed the usual process and handed Jon that interesting project.

> Carl parked his new SUV in the usual spot and walked into the back foyer of his office block. He had spent a sleepless night going over the events of the day before and wondering if he had imagined the cool looks and tension in the air. He had arrived feeling tired, gloomy and more than a bit annoyed with his team. As he looked up he saw the deputy CEO, Phil, watching him.
>
> 'What's up?' Phil asked. 'You look as if a storm cloud is about to burst over you.' After Carl summed up the previous day's events Phil replied, 'Well today you have a choice – put on your best face or let everyone know you are in a bad mood and take it out on the first unlucky person to step into your office.'

Hopefully, Carl will pull himself together and start the day on a more positive note. Everyone gets in a bad mood sometimes, but how they handle themselves when they do is what counts. It is not easy to overcome a personal feeling. Carl needs to take ownership and stop blaming other people for how he feels.

Many leaders do not recognise the negative impacts on morale and productivity when they lose their cool easily, treat people dismissively or behave badly in countless other ways. Stride into the office in the morning without greeting people? The message received is that the team isn't important enough to merit a simple hello. Or that the leader is arrogant, or both. Ask the team for their views then tinker with a smartphone while they are giving them? They get the message that the boss does not really care about their ideas. Or that the decision is already made, or both.

Poor demeanour indicates disinterest or a lack of respect. It doesn't matter that the leader did not intend to convey this – that they were busy or worried about a problem that just came up. Treat one or two people with disdain and everyone will feel diminished. Civility, on the other hand, is a good platform for positive interactions and the development of trusting and supportive relationships. Treating people professionally at all times, regardless of personal feelings of like or dislike, are behaviours that are noticed by every member of the team.

There are few things more destructive of team morale than favouritism or prejudice. The perception that the boss is favouring some people and leaving others in the cold is just as damaging as the actual behaviour. Consider Carl's situation – he felt he had to make a quick decision and chose Jon, but that is not how the team saw it. They thought he was playing favourites. It would have been even worse if, on the next day, he had reacted to his own feelings and taken them out on the team. Fortunately, Phil was around to remind Carl that the ability to self-manage is a key skill for leaders.

Clearly, the demand for leaders to possess sophisticated interpersonal skills has never been greater. Unfortunately, people like Carl often start in their leadership roles with little preparation. Post-school education still focuses mainly on the technical side of jobs and not much at all on the challenges of working with people. How much of your professional or technical training was spent in preparing you to work with or manage others? Many organisations provide in-house management training, but sometimes first-time managers are thrown in at the deep end. It's often a case of sink or swim.

The surest foundation for good interpersonal skills are:

- ✓ self-knowledge
- ✓ the ability to self-manage
- ✓ empathy.

If you are aware of your own attitudes and emotions, you can anticipate how you will react in particular circumstances. Even when your hot buttons are pressed you can prepare yourself better and remain in control. Empathy is the ability to put yourself in the shoes of another person, and see things from their perspective. It is easier to work with people when you understand their reality. And of course, they will respond better to you if they feel you understand where they are coming from, even if you do not agree on all points.

These capabilities are components of emotional intelligence. Without a doubt leaders need emotional intelligence as much as they need the ability to think analytically and strategically. In your role as leader there will be many situations where you need all that you can muster. You might have a colleague or team member who is, at the best of times, difficult to get along with. Or your team might be under the pressure of tight deadlines or limited resources, an uncertain future or major changes. Emotions are always a part of the picture, and at times they will run high. Managing difficult relationships and keeping people calm and focused are all part of the role.

Chapter 7 contains many suggestions about how to behave in an emotionally intelligent way, to manage difficult relationships and to cope with other stresses that come with your leadership role.

Over to you

You have made a conscious choice to step into a leadership role. However, the first weeks and months can be a shock – if you are like most other new leaders, you have had little preparation for it. It's time to make some plans and put them into practice. Put simply, the way forward is in building a team of willing collaborators who are very clear about what they intend to achieve together.

But how? You now know a little about the three knowledge and capability domains that are critical to your success as a leader:

- focusing the individual and team effort so that you are adding value to your organisation
- motivating everyone to work to their potential
- creating a positive social climate that ensures trust and collaborative work relationships.

While we can treat these as separate domains, in reality, a leader needs to attend to all three simultaneously. Consider Frank, our team leader of the 'fresh and frozen' department in a branch of an independent supermarket chain. Frank has focus – he knows what he wants the team to do and is very conscientious in his efforts to improve standards. But he is frustrated because people are not cooperating enough. He will get better results when he does more to engage the team and build a positive social climate. Along with Margo and Carl, we will return to him later on in the book to see if he has rounded out his leadership by increasing his capability in all three domains.

Chapter 3
Your leadership style

As we look ahead into the next century,
leaders will be those who empower others.

Bill Gates

In this chapter ...

You will see that effective leadership is also about your leadership style –
how you build relationships and use your power and influence. The style
of leadership that has the best potential to build a team of people who
are engaged in their work is an empowering style. We will contrast this
with other approaches that are less effective. The likely consequences of
the empowering leadership style for productivity, employee satisfaction
and other worthwhile outcomes will also be explored.

Engaging your team

You now know what you need to do to build a productive team. In this
chapter we will consider how to go about doing it, in other words, the best
ways to communicate and interact with your team on a daily basis. The way
you connect with people is critical because this is how you make them feel
included, safe, in control and optimistic. It is about creating a positive space
where people can flourish.

In the previous chapter we outlined the behaviour typical of effective leaders,
explaining what they do to build high-performing teams. We concluded that
the best leaders do three things: they maintain focus on the things that

matter, they motivate and reward the team, and they create a positive social climate. Effective leadership is the sum of all these things. But if one aspect of leadership behaviour binds them all, it is a style of leading that engages the team in their work.

How important is employee engagement? People who are engaged are more productive. Workplaces where a higher proportion of workers are engaged get better results across several criteria including profitability, customer loyalty, quality, safety, wellbeing and discretionary effort. There is now proof of this. Over many years the Gallup organisation has conducted regular surveys of numerous people and workplaces across the globe. Their main conclusion is unequivocal – workplace engagement is vital for achieving sustainable results for organisations, communities and nations.

So, if the level of employee engagement is the test of a good leader, how well are leaders performing? The evidence will shock you. The latest Gallup[10] survey results show that only 13% of employees worldwide are engaged at work. Another 63% fall into the 'not engaged' category, while a third group of 24% surveyed are 'actively disengaged'. Of course, leadership is not the only factor associated with engagement but it is an important one. So on this evidence we are forced to conclude that leaders as a whole are not performing at all well. This amounts to an enormous waste of human energy and creativity, and a loss of opportunity for organisations to deliver better outcomes to their many stakeholders across all sectors of society.

You are reading this book because you intend to be a leader with the credibility and influence to create a team of willing followers who care about their work and want to achieve results as much as you do. You want your team to be fully engaged and you hope to avoid the many pitfalls that others have apparently fallen prey to. This is where your leadership style comes into its own – the way that you interact with people and craft trusting, supportive relationships.

Some of your questions about leadership style might include these:

- What is the best way to interact with people?
- Should I be friendly or a bit more distant?
- How do I build trust?

- How do I go about including people and making them feel valued?
- Can I get people to be more creative or innovative?
- How can I get people to share their ideas or help one another?
- How do I get people to be frank and open with me?

One of your main goals as a leader should be to align your leadership style with all the things you do to focus effort, energise and motivate the team, and build a positive social climate. It is a complete package that will bring you success. You will find many of the answers to your questions about how to do this in this chapter.

Two ways of interacting

Think about your everyday interactions at work. Do you like to spend a lot of time with your team? Do you often meet up with individuals and groups, talking things through, discussing methods and results, puzzling over problems and dilemmas and rejigging resources and timeframes? Do you genuinely listen and take the team's ideas into account as you do so? Are you comfortable in complimenting a person on their work or results? Do you regularly provide feedback, noting things that are going well, or giving a bit of advice to get someone back on track? Is your door usually open, and if so, do people seem happy enough to come to you for advice? Do you see yourself as more of a coach than a supervisor?

If your answer to most of these questions is 'yes', you like to bring people along with you, giving them encouragement and the room to grow. It is an empowering style of interaction.

Or do you, on the other hand, like to keep things more formal, taking your responsibility to regulate the work and monitor performance very seriously? Do you see yourself as the person most capable of making plans and decisions, finding that the place runs more smoothly when you are at the helm? Do you think that some people are not particularly trustworthy around valuable resources or company property? Are you concerned that the team might ease off or become a bit more careless when it is out of your sight? Do you see yourself as more of a supervisor than a coach?

If your answer to most of these questions is 'yes', you like to be in command and keep a close eye on things. It is a controlling style of interaction. We can compare the styles in terms of the degree of social distance or formality between the leader and the team members. Empowering leaders reduce the social distance and behave like advisers or coaches. Controlling leaders set themselves above the team and behave like monitors or overseers.

The above descriptions of the empowering and controlling styles are fairly extreme. If you think of them as representing two ends of a continuum then the style of most leaders would be a little away from either end and perhaps more towards the middle. Think about the leadership style that characterises you at the moment. Where would you place yourself on the continuum?

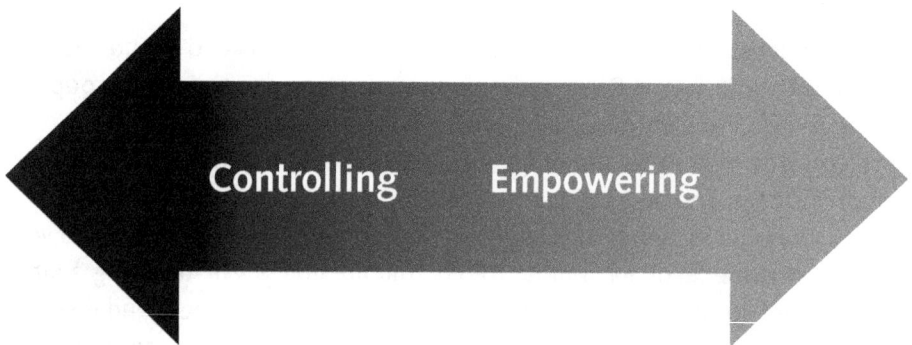

Controlling   Empowering

In the following scenario we meet Frank's boss, Kaitlin, who has managed the suburban supermarket for several years. Kaitlin is aware that Frank is a little frustrated in his efforts to improve food handling standards and that he is unsure of what to try next. She has arranged to meet with him later in the day, and has been reflecting on her early days as a new leader with a different employer, the country's leading supermarket chain.

Kaitlin remembered the day she arrived back in the department after an enlightening week at the corporation's course for new leaders. (Unlike her current organisation, they had a big training budget!) Before the course she had been concerned about the mediocre results of her team and baffled by their lack of initiative and resistance to change. The course had given her some answers and now she was all fired up and keen to put her new ideas into practice. She realised that her style of leadership would have to change for her team to do better. Give them more latitude to explore different options, encourage people to share ideas, and ask them to come to her with solutions, not problems. She had also decided to get out of her office and try to be more approachable.

Kaitlin did not expect what happened next. Instead of responding with enthusiasm, most members of the team seemed to draw back. After a quiet word with one of her trusted colleagues it dawned on her. They were suspicious. The boss had lost the plot. Why this sudden change from her usual approach? She used to know what she wanted and made sure that everyone else knew it too. No ifs or buts. Would she get over it and return to her old, familiar self?

Before the leadership course, Kaitlin's style of leadership was formal and controlling. She made most of the decisions and showed little interest in getting her team involved. This stifled their energy and creativity, because it encouraged them to sit back and wait to be told. No wonder results were mediocre! The leadership course provided Kaitlin with some important insights into the impact of her behaviour on the team. She now understood that her people would perform better if they were empowered with more responsibility and autonomy.

The dilemma for leaders like Kaitlin is that it can take some time for team members to adjust to a new style and a different set of expectations. She had not anticipated the confusion and natural resistance that her change in style would generate. The message here is not that empowering people is a bad thing. On the contrary, there is overwhelming evidence that this style of management works much better than more controlling approaches. It may just take some time to put it into practice and for others to accept it.

Influence and power

Another way to compare the styles of controlling and empowering leaders is to look at how they use influence. Every leader needs influence to shape the action. For example, one leader wants people to spend more time talking to customers and showing them the merchandise. Another wants the team to be more creative in their problem solving. To have influence is to have impact – that is, the capacity to bring people around to do things that they might not otherwise have done.

Influence is a form of social currency, generating drive and energy. It is what leaders use to lift the team's performance, change behaviour and direction, and mould culture and attitudes. Building influence and using it wisely are hallmarks of good leadership. When done well this brings out the best in people and creates a climate that is both productive and rewarding.

Where does your influence come from? Influence is based on the power at your disposal. Power is a form of leverage. If you have power, you can use it to hold sway over others. Potentially, you have access to many forms of power. Some are quite direct and transparent when used, such as a command to do things in a particular way. For example, a leader might give a specific direction to team members to spend more time on the shop floor and interact with customers as soon as they enter the store.

Power can also be more indirect and subtle in use. For example, the leader who wants the team to be more creative could improve skills by providing coaching. They could also share more of the planning and decision making, encourage collaboration and shared learning, and ensure that creativity is appropriately rewarded.

Two aspects of power are on show in these examples. There is the actual source of the power and choices made by the leader about how to use it. In the first case, the source of power is the store manager's formal position and the authority that comes with it. She has used it in the form of a direct command. The power used by the second leader is based on several sources, including her expertise, position of authority and ability to communicate. The first leader uses the power in a directive way, the second uses hers to mould the team.

Each power source has advantages as well as limitations. A direct command works well when you want people to, for example, do fairly concrete things like spend more time on the shop floor. It also has advantages when tight coordination is needed or response times have to be quick. However, direct commands are inappropriate in situations where you want people to be more creative.

Using influence and power

Leaders with an empowering leadership style use influence in a very different way from those with a controlling style. The way that controlling leaders use power and influence is shown in the following diagram. They rely heavily on the formal authority that comes with their position and tend to stand over people. You will also notice that there are real consequences in terms of what the controlling leader gets back from the team – people generally do only what they have to and this usually means mediocre results and low engagement.

Controlling leaders

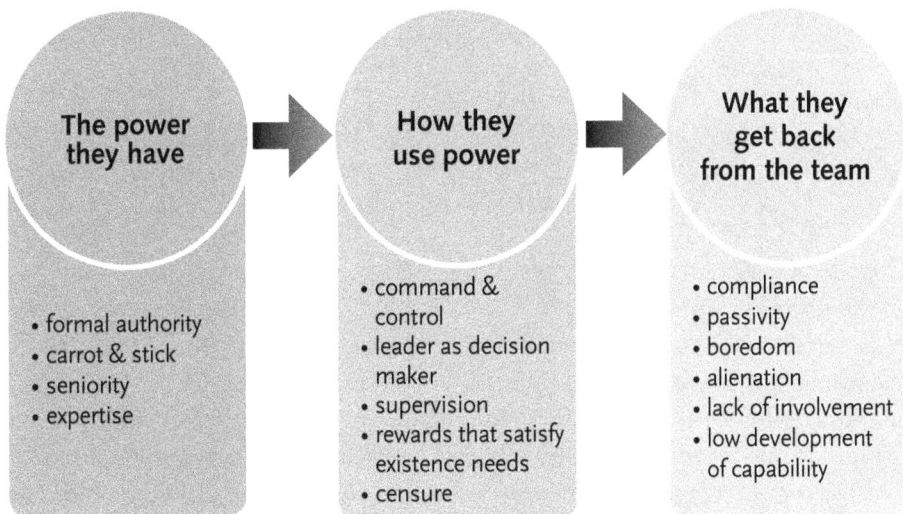

The power they have	How they use power	What they get back from the team
• formal authority • carrot & stick • seniority • expertise	• command & control • leader as decision maker • supervision • rewards that satisfy existence needs • censure	• compliance • passivity • boredom • alienation • lack of involvement • low development of capabiliity

In our earlier example, Frank relies heavily on his formal authority and expertise. He tries to influence the team through direct commands but gets little back from them. At best they comply when he is watching.

We can contrast this with the very different approach of empowering leaders. The diagram shows that they rely more on their expertise and a positive team culture, and use it to build team capability. As a result they get much more back from the team.

Empowering leaders

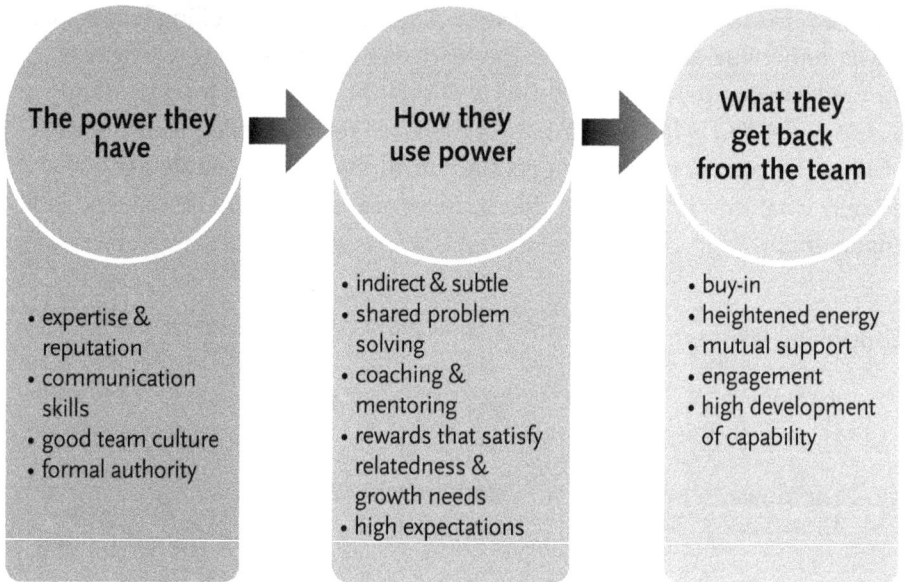

The power they have	How they use power	What they get back from the team
• expertise & reputation • communication skills • good team culture • formal authority	• indirect & subtle • shared problem solving • coaching & mentoring • rewards that satisfy relatedness & growth needs • high expectations	• buy-in • heightened energy • mutual support • engagement • high development of capability

The use of the term 'empowerment' was first used for work settings by Rosabeth Moss Kanter[11] in 1977. She saw that when people were empowered, or allowed to have control over their decisions and actions, more could be accomplished. She advocated that leaders should delegate responsibility, encourage the team to participate in making decisions and give them the resources they needed to do the job well. In her view this was the best way to build the total capacity of the organisation. Leadership behaviour that was controlling, on the other hand, rendered most others powerless and unable to act effectively. In other words, leaders who monopolised power placed limits on what they were able to do through their teams.

Consider Kaitlin's situation. Initially she had a controlling leadership style where she used her authority to make most of the decisions and supervise closely. As a consequence, the team was passive, compliant and disengaged. Their performance was mediocre and they showed a lack of initiative.

Fortunately, Kaitlin had the insight to recognise that this had come about because of her own behaviour. As a leader adopting the empowering style Kaitlin started to build her power in ways suggested in the table below.

Source of power	As used with the empowering style
Expertise & reputation	• set standards • refine work processes • guide, mentor & upskill team members • encourage professionalism & ethical behaviour
Knowledge of company systems, processes & access to senior leaders	• obtain resources for the team (e.g. funding, staff) • gain support & expertise from others • obtain visibility for the team & its achievements
Communication skills	• foster a climate of openness, information sharing & all-way communication • participate in key discussions with colleagues & those more senior
Inclusive team culture	• get buy-in & commitment to team goals • use success stories to lift sights & expectations • build confidence in individual & team capacity to go 'from good to great'
Personal warmth	• show genuine interest in individual needs & aspirations • be empathic & a good listener • create a climate of inclusiveness
Corporate & professional networks	• extend access to quality advice & expertise • build reputation with professionals in & outside the organisation • source developmental opportunities for team members

The empowering leadership style leaves team members feeling involved, valued and satisfied. The controlling style, on the other hand, leaves people feeling out in the cold and, at best, only somewhat satisfied. By empowering others you increase your team's skills and capabilities, and generate commitment, energy and creativity. Think of the empowering style as essentially a power-sharing and power-extending arrangement, with you at the apex. Your formal authority still counts but it settles into the background and you come across to your team more as a colleague than an overseer.

Think about the sources of power that you currently use. Where are your strengths? Are you relying too heavily on your formal power? What sources of power do you need to develop so that your capacity to engage your team is greater?

Two styles of leadership in action

How would employees typically respond to you if you adopted the controlling leadership style? Or the empowering style?

Let us assume your style is at the extreme end of controlling and you rely heavily on your formal power. Essentially, this means you act like top dog and expect people to fall into line. How do they react? For one thing, they are careful to stay on your good side, and avoid doing anything that you might not like. Your style of leadership is a constant reminder to them that you have the power to hire and fire, reward or punish. In every encounter with you, they are very conscious of the consequences if they do not measure up in your eyes. This makes them cautious, fearful of making a mistake and quick to cover up any problems.

How are the relationships in a team like this? Straightforward, but not great. In the main they are one-to-one arrangements between you and each person. You dominate in most work-related conversations and show little interest in their ideas. In fact, you usually decide most things yourself and tell each person what they have to do. We can hardly describe it as at team at all. Naturally friendships develop among the people in your team, impressions are shared, concerns aired and ways to resist your authority devised (out of your earshot, of course). But these relationships are not about better work methods or improving productivity – realistically, they are for helping each other to survive.

Now contrast this with the empowering style. In adopting this approach you rely primarily on your expertise and use it to advise and coach team members regarding quality, standards and suitable work methods. Communication is freer and there is discussion around how to solve problems together. As you develop in your role you supplement this source of influence by building your knowledge about how organisational systems and processes work, improving your communication skills and expanding your professional networks, among other things. All of these enable you to do more for and with your team.

How do people react to you? In most situations, very well. They appreciate having a leader who listens to their problems and ideas, and who is more interested in helping them improve than telling them off for getting something wrong. Most enjoy participating in team meetings and helping to solve problems. The openness and supportive atmosphere creates a climate of trust – just what you need to get even more collaboration and buy-in. Naturally, the team's culture develops in a way that supports your shared objectives.

It is easy to see that as an empowering leader you can be closer to your team than if you choose a controlling style. It provides more scope for people to mould their jobs according to their skills, interests and experience. And it gives them more say over how they do their work and consult with you about things that matter to them. Genuine teamwork is much more likely.

Which leader gets the best results?

Does the controlling leadership style deliver results? Yes, in a limited way. Things do get done, but the chances of achieving anything better than mediocre results are poor. Quality suffers because people do not feel free to act, and productivity is even poorer when the boss's back is turned.

Improvements in efficiency and work methods are therefore unlikely. Unlikely, that is, unless the leader comes up with them. But there is plenty of evidence to suggest that some of the best innovations come from the people actually doing the work, and then only if they are actively encouraged and supported. If the leader behaves like an overseer this won't happen because people fear getting into trouble if they try anything new.

Most modern industries and organisations function more happily, collaboratively and productively under conditions that empower because employees are engaged, interested and are not afraid to use their initiative. When people are consulted, listened to and given a choice they are far more likely to willingly cooperate. The productivity benefits are considerable.

This might seem obvious to us today but not so long ago the prevailing leadership style was very controlling. The turnaround began during the late 1930s with some carefully executed experiments comparing leadership styles[12]. Adolescent boys 'worked' in groups making masks and the like under the leadership of one of the experimenters. When acting as an autocrat he told the boys what to do and how to do it, dominated, criticised, and disrupted play by changing things around from time to time. When playing the role of an empowering leader he allowed the group to decide among themselves about goals and work methods while offering help and encouragement when it was needed.

The differences between the groups were striking. Under the controlling leadership style the boys lost initiative, became discontented, broke tools or destroyed work, were sometimes aggressive towards one another and held little interest in group goals. In contrast, the boys with the empowering leader were much more friendly towards one another, were open and cooperative and reported enjoying the experience much more than they did when in the other group.

These findings have since been confirmed many times – people are more focused and productive when actively supported by a leader with an empowering style and when planning their own goals and work methods. They are also more likely to report a high quality of work life (QWL).

QWL refers to the degree of satisfaction and fulfilment a person derives from their job. Organisations that provide a good QWL are typically high on the list of desirable ones to work for. Here is a list of items that are generally regarded as important for QWL:

- ✓ participation in making decisions about their work
- ✓ an atmosphere of trust and openness
- ✓ being acknowledged and appropriately rewarded for effort and results
- ✓ having opportunities to grow and develop
- ✓ a work environment that is friendly, pleasant and balanced.

Are these high on your QWL agenda? If they are, chances are that your team members will value them as much.

Other experiments during the 1940s showed that similar principles apply to organisational change. With war-time food shortages, the US government wanted housewives to alter habits and tastes by using more 'variety meats'. Official cajoling and entreaties had not worked. Kurt Lewin and the famous anthropologist Margaret Mead ran a series of experiments similar to the focus groups we use today[13]. They discovered that women were willing to change when they were presented with relevant information and collectively made decisions about how they would put it into practice.

The idea that people are more willing to change if they are involved in the decision making was later tested by Lewin in manufacturing organisations – production increased when workers on the shop floor were invited to participate in devising better work methods. These days, no leader in his or her right mind would attempt to impose a change on people if there was scope to involve them in the planning. But as you can see, this idea is fairly new. Sixty or so years ago leaders made all the decisions, leaving little room for employee participation. Since then, the leader shift – from overseer to colleague – has been transformational.

The human side of enterprise

In those early years many great management pioneers helped to advance our thinking on leadership. Most were academics or consultants with industry contacts, so were well aware that performance was generally poor against most criteria. Their motives were mixed – to increase productivity and to make workplaces more congenial, harmonious and better for the workers. There is not enough room here to describe the situation as it was a century ago but suffice to say that few workplaces were efficient or productive, free of industrial conflict or pleasant places to work.

Kurt Lewin was an early pioneer in the movement to humanise the workplace. Even before his experiments on leadership style, he was an influential thinker who went on to establish firm links between higher productivity and giving workers the freedom to plan their own tasks. He believed that everyone should have work that was fulfilling and added to their 'life value'. More than anyone, Lewin believed that people could transform their lives through meaningful work.

Prior to Lewin, Mary Parker Follett[14] in the 1920s was an admired advocate for a new style of management based on collaborative relationships and mutual trust, less bureaucracy, and more focus on common needs and interests. She believed that workers should be empowered because they were valuable assets with knowledge and expertise, capable of making a greater contribution to organisations and society. Although she was well ahead of her time, Follett's ideas gradually filtered through and have influenced many others since.

By the 1930s and 1940s, industrial psychologists were focusing on the everyday feelings and experiences of ordinary workers. This began with a series of experiments to increase worker productivity by manipulating lighting levels in a General Electric factory. In the process, Elton Mayo[15] and his colleagues 'discovered' that workers responded more to the opportunity to socialise with the experimenters than to changes in the physical environment. They were incredulous at first. Productivity increased when the experimenters walked around, chatted and were nice to people.

It opened a can of worms. Here was 'proof' that people had social needs and they brought them to work! Who would have thought it? What other human needs might be hidden under the drudgery and monotony of the typical factory job?

This important experiment, known as the Hawthorne Studies, stimulated a new interest in human needs, including the contribution of Clayton Alderfer, whose ERG theory was explained in Chapter 2 of this book. It also alerted others to the main reasons behind the problems besetting industry – unfulfilling work and powerlessness.

Some 50 years ago, Douglas McGregor brought much of the earlier thinking together in *The Human Side of Enterprise* (1960)[16], in which he wrote about the high level of industrial disharmony and conflict that was limiting productivity and stifling innovation. He identified the source of the problems to be jobs that dehumanised and the way in which people were managed – in particular, the controlling leadership style that was prevalent at the time.

His message to the leaders of industry was simple but powerful – if you want to improve the situation you must change the way you lead and manage. Treat people differently and they will behave differently! However, he could see how difficult this would be because taking control was not just a way of doing things, it was deeply embedded in the thinking of most managers of the time. They genuinely believed that standing over people was the only way to get results. As McGregor saw it, attitudes would need to change.

These days we know a lot more about how to influence people. Even so, managers are often impatient for quick responses or changes in behaviours from their teams. Think of Frank who just wants people to do things his way. If he keeps it up he will get people further offside. Results will improve if he changes his attitude and encourages some buy-in.

Theory X and Theory Y

McGregor contrasted the prevailing managerial attitudes about workers (authoritarian attitudes which he labelled 'Theory X') with a different set (his 'Theory Y' or egalitarian attitudes) that would support a more enlightened approach to leadership.

Theory X	Theory Y
Most people dislike work & will avoid it to the extent possible.	Work is as natural as play – people like or dislike it depending on the conditions that management imposes.
Workers must be continually coerced, controlled & threatened with punishment to get work done.	External control is not the only way – people exercise self-control to reach objectives if they are trusted to.
Workers have little or no ambition.	People want the opportunity to improve their position & build a career.
Most prefer to avoid responsibility.	Under the right conditions people will accept responsibility rather than avoid it.
Security is their main preoccupation.	People seek to satisfy many complex needs, including self-esteem, achievement & growth.

Put yourself in the shoes of those Theory X managers. If you really believed that people dislike work, avoid responsibility, and so on, then of course you would want to take control, watching closely for signs of slackness, checking everything for errors and not trusting people when they are out of your sight. If, on the other hand, your attitudes were more like Theory Y, you would expect people to work on without having to be told, and be comfortable in giving them responsibility and the opportunity to develop.

(You get) as good as you give

The breakthrough thinking from McGregor was his realisation that attitudes and behaviours are strongly linked. His enduring message for us is this –

when it comes to managing people, your way of thinking strongly influences your behaviour, and it is your behaviour that others respond to. This was the concept of 'self-fulfilling prophecy' applied to management. Here is an example of how it works:

At drinks on Friday with the other managers, Carl was on again about the mediocre performance and 'don't care' attitude of some of his planners.

'There is a group of them who have been here for too long, just waiting out the days until their retirement. They have no idea about modern commercial development and are not interested in finding out. I just give them the routine development applications to keep them busy.'

Phil looked at him long and hard before asking, 'Well, how are you going to staff the new town centre development project that is about to kick off if you don't use all the talent in your team? Don't write those people off – I have known them for a long time – they have done some great work in the past. Give them a challenge, let them back in and show some confidence in what they can do.'

The point is, of course, that our beliefs, attitudes and assumptions show through and have a real impact on how others respond to us. Carl seems blind to the impact of his own attitudes on the behaviour of the planners but once again Phil has stepped in with a bit of informal mentoring when it was needed. If we think that a particular person (or team) is creative or resourceful, we convey that to them in one way or another. And a lot of that communication is non-verbal. It might be very subtle, and we may not even be aware of it, but somehow, the message gets through.

Read more about self-fulfilling prophecy in the story of the highly intelligent rats. This story is based on some careful experiments showing that attitudes really do make a difference. They are not just hidden and private. Experiments like these have also explored the damaging effects of stereotyping and prejudices in many social contexts. For example, hiring decisions are affected by negative attitudes about racial or cultural background and gender. It follows that people can change their behaviour if they are prepared to reflect on their attitudes and change their thinking.

The highly intelligent rats

In the early 1960s Professor Robert Rosenthal told his social psychology students that he had bred a strain of super-intelligent rats that could run mazes quickly[17]. Their task, he added, was to train the rats in maze running. Half the group was told that their rat was one of the bright ones, while the other half was told they had a rat with average ability. In fact, the rats were allocated randomly and all were normal – nothing special about them at all.

How did the rats perform? The rats believed to be bright did significantly better than the rats believed to have average ability. How could this be? The professor surmised that students with the supposedly bright rats communicated higher expectations to them. But how? The answer comes from looking at the students' behaviour and attitudes. To quote the professor, students who thought they were working with bright rats 'liked them better and found them more pleasant'. They felt relaxed and treated their rats 'more gently' and were 'more enthusiastic' about the experiment than the other students.

This is the same Professor Rosenthal who, with Lenore Jacobson, ran a groundbreaking experiment with school teachers[18]. They were told that certain of the children in their class were intellectual bloomers and should be expected to show accelerated development. Of course, the students were allocated randomly to the 'bloomer' and 'other' groups. Over the school year, on average the 'bloomers' did develop to a significantly greater degree than the other students. It wasn't about the amount of time spent with each child, but the quality of the interaction. Oh! And like the students with the 'bright' rats, the teachers found the 'bloomers' to be more appealing, affectionate and well-adjusted.

These stories tell us a great deal. Most importantly, people respond to the messages they receive from others, whether these messages are overt or very subtle. Treat someone as if they are clumsy or inept, and that's likely the way they will behave. There is a lesson here for leaders – treat your people like responsible, competent adults, and watch their performance improve.

If you truly believe that people work better when they are trusted with important decisions, and your organisation has a culture that favours an empowering style of leadership, then you should fit well in this environment. On the other hand, if you tend towards Theory X attitudes and your words of encouragement are contradicted by your non-verbal signals, people will notice. You would undermine yourself by putting on a show of support when it was clear to all around that it was just an act.

Leadership style today

Over the past 50 years we have seen a marked shift away from the controlling style and towards the empowering style of leadership – at least in theory. The empowering style has been advocated through management training courses, degrees in management, and in just about every book or article on managing people written during that time. Numerous managers have been exposed to the idea. So why are the surveys indicating that so many employees are not engaged or are actively disengaged? Clearly, something does not add up.

Let's be blunt about this. Many leaders, perhaps the majority, are not doing enough to make empowerment a reality. They might know about it, or even talk about it, but they are not doing enough of it. We will look at some of the possible reasons for this, but first, we need to revisit the idea of leadership style.

The empowering style of leadership is known to be better than the controlling style because it is based on Theory Y attitudes. As you have already seen, many leaders have the view that people are attracted to tasks that interest them, are prepared to take responsibility, contribute their expertise and develop their skills. They get a very good response from their teams in most situations. On the other hand, the controlling style is based on Theory X attitudes. Leaders who have these attitudes repress involvement and creativity. At best, they get mediocre results from their teams.

Leaders with either the empowering or controlling styles are proactive in the way they turn their beliefs into actions. But we have already identified a gap between attitudes and action. Some leaders are passive and are not acting like either empowering or controlling leaders. This implies that there are at least two more styles of leadership to explore.

We can do this with the aid of a diagram.

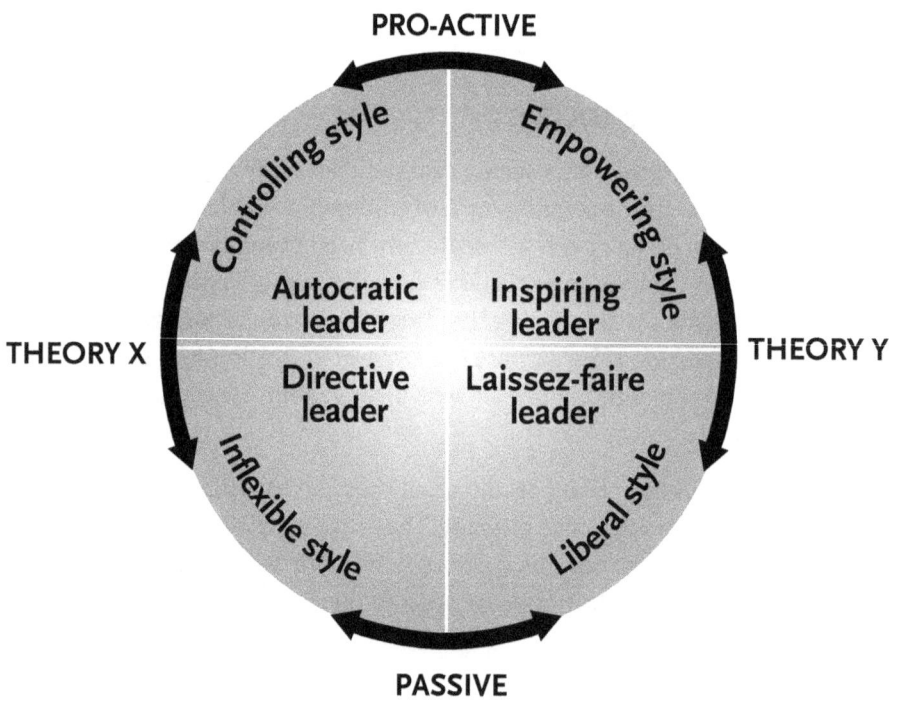

The diagram depicts four types of leader, each with a characteristic leadership style as follows:

- inspiring leader with an empowering style
- autocratic leader with a controlling style
- laissez-faire leader with a liberal style
- directive leader with an inflexible style.

So far, we have talked about the empowering and controlling styles of leadership and in the diagram have now added their leadership tags. Inspiring leaders have an empowering style based on their egalitarian (Theory Y) attitudes. They are proactive in the ways they put them into action with their teams. Autocratic leaders are also proactive but the attitudes they work from are Theory X and they use a controlling style.

We also have two new leader types: laissez-faire and directive leaders.

Directive leaders

Directive leaders have similar attitudes about people to autocratic leaders, but they are less overt in how they action them. They like to be in charge and rely heavily on their formal authority. They are also fixed in their ideas about how things should be done and expect the team to fall into line. But unlike autocratic leaders they take a more hands-off approach. They monitor progress, but generally from a distance, preferring charts, spreadsheets and emails to close personal supervision. They are most likely to speak to the team when activity falls beneath acceptable levels or standards. These interactions are therefore usually about finding fault or issuing reprimands. We could describe their leadership style as inflexible.

Autocratic and directive leaders have this in common – they are all about having the first and final word on 'who', 'what' and 'how' (these leaders rarely feel the need to explain the 'why'). They believe that the leader's job is to control the action and make sure things are done according to plan (their plan). This causes those on the receiving end to be motivated by fear or resentment, and as one way of fighting back, to often do the minimum amount of work that they can get away with.

You will recall from earlier in this chapter that Kaitlin was planning to meet with Frank to discuss his leadership. Here is a brief part of their conversation.

> 'I've got the diploma,' continued Frank. 'I know how it's supposed to be done. Why can't they just get on with it and do what I tell them? It's not complicated, or am I missing something?'
>
> 'Perhaps you are,' replied Kaitlin. 'You can't control everything, and you are not there all the time. Is there any scope for you to consult with the team and encourage them to take more responsibility? People want to be listened to and have some say in how they do their jobs.'
>
> 'Perhaps,' replied Frank, 'but they don't have my expertise, so what if standards start to slip again?'
>
> 'You might be surprised,' she said. 'Would you like to talk through a few things that you could try?'

As a leader, Frank is somewhere between autocratic and directive. Whether he realises it or not, his attitudes are more Theory X than Theory Y. That is why he tends to be inflexible and controlling. As you can see, Kaitlin has decided to coach Frank so that he loosens the controls, and moves towards a more empowering style of leadership. From her own experience, she is sure that his team will be more willing to change their food handling practices if he can do this.

Laissez-faire leaders

Laissez-faire leaders are similar to inspiring leaders in that they have Theory Y attitudes, which are often strongly held. The difference is that they tend to stand back from the team and are quite liberal in allowing people to go about their daily business. Laissez-faire leaders use their formal authority to do the planning and organising and are often good networkers who are well-regarded in their organisation. However, they stop short of doing many of the things that would actually inspire the team to greater achievement. Perhaps this is because they have ample confidence in the commitment and capability of their staff and believe that most people work best when left alone to get on with it.

So while their relationships are cordial, laissez-faire leaders are relatively inactive when it comes to providing feedback and encouragement, taking an interest in the career aspirations of team members, creating opportunities for them to develop, or showing concern for their general wellbeing. Because the liberal style of interacting is relatively detached, uninvolved and unengaging, it often results in a lack of team cohesion and missed opportunities for excellence or innovation.

Margo, in the physiotherapy department, is veering towards the laissez-faire leadership style. Here is a little more of her story:

Within a week or two of starting the job, Margo realises that all of the physiotherapists in her team are experienced, skilled and dedicated, and used to doing their work with little direction. This comes as a relief because the volume of her admin and case management work is far greater than she had expected. As things are she can spend the bulk of her time organising the files and keeping things ship-shape, rather than spending time in the therapy rooms.

In fact, during her last few visits she felt a little awkward and useless. Everyone was working busily with their patients and paid her little attention. She was relieved to get back to her office.

After her recent conversation with Anthony, she can also see that fighting for resources, like new equipment, will be a big part of the job. Networking does not come naturally to her, but that is what she has decided to do, for the sake of the team.

With the best of intentions, Margo is taking a hands-off approach, believing that the physiotherapists work effectively when left alone and that she will be more useful if she directs her time elsewhere. Of course, the networking and administration are important but without realising it Margo, like most laissez-faire leaders, is placing limits on what she and the team are capable of achieving.

Why are there so few inspiring leaders?

We have seen a shift towards egalitarian attitudes but the emergence of a leadership style where they are proactively applied appears to have lagged behind. As a result we have too few inspiring leaders and probably too many laissez-faire ones. Why? What is the problem?

Putting theory into practice is not easy. It is one thing to know that you should, for example, include the team in decision making or delegate more responsibility, but quite another to know how to do it. We could say the same for many of the things that good leaders do, like on-the-job training, giving regular feedback on performance and encouraging the team to take more initiative. As we have already noted, one reason is because many leaders are not well prepared for their roles.

Also for many new leaders, the liberal style of the laissez-faire leader is not a conscious choice. It is more of a default, the path they take with the best of intentions. In their minds, team leaders are for organising and allocating the work, managing conflict, and keeping senior management off their backs.

With Margo, for example, there was probably no defining moment when she decided to take the laissez-faire path. She simply responded to the situation as she saw it. Margo thinks like many people leading teams of highly skilled professionals, such as accountants, nurses, teachers and lawyers – their teams are educated and trained to a high level, freeing the leader to tackle the other tasks piling up on their desks.

Leaders are action oriented – they like to keep things moving along and have little time for reflection. Even if they do, most have some blind spots when it comes to their behaviour and impact on other people. Carl, for example, does not realise that members of his team think that he plays favourites. In his own mind he allocates work to the people most capable of doing it, but some believe that his decisions are unfair.

It is hard to be objective about yourself and it can come as a shock to learn that you are not coming across to others in the way you thought you were. Sometimes we simply do not see the gap.

We need feedback on our behaviour to keep check on how we are performing. Feedback comes to us in many forms. Reflecting on our own feelings and behaviour is one of the best sources but unless we open up to suggestions from other people, we run the risk of missing something useful or important.

Here are some suggestions for opening yourself up to realistic feedback:

- ✓ Notice your own patterns – the people, tasks and situations that you warm to, and those that sap your energy.
- ✓ Notice when you overreact or have an unexpected response to people or events and try to understand why.
- ✓ Emotions can be confusing, so name them and notice which ones come up in particular situations.
- ✓ Get the most out of your organisation's performance appraisal, especially 360° feedback if they use it.
- ✓ Seek out feedback from others and regard it as a gift (including criticism) even if you think it is not true or warranted.
- ✓ If you like writing, keep a reflective journal of your experiences as a new leader.
- ✓ Find a mentor more senior to yourself and meet with them often.

There are other reasons beyond the direct control of leaders as to why so many people are not engaged at work. In the next chapter we will cover some factors from history that have held organisations back. It can be hard for leaders to use an empowering style when the culture does not support it.

In addition, modern work pressures can create barriers that make it difficult for leaders to engage their teams. For instance, threats of redundancy and demanding schedules can put relationships under stress. In brief, many factors help to explain lower levels of employee engagement than is desirable.

Over to you

The style of leadership that you choose is possibly the most important decision you will make. Only one of the four styles covered in this chapter will deliver the level of employee empowerment needed for consistently good results and high levels of job satisfaction among team members. That style is, of course, the empowering style of the inspiring leader. To adopt this style you not only need to have egalitarian (Theory Y) attitudes, but also a determination to put them into practice.

Inspiring leaders understand it is important for people to be emotionally invested in the team and the job. They believe that people will do their best when the conditions are right and respond to opportunities to develop and grow. They communicate high expectations and motivate the team to achieve high performance and quality.

As a goal for you, being an inspiring leader might seem to be a long way away. But think about the behaviour behind the label, what it really means in a practical sense, and it will seem more achievable. Inspiring leaders engage others in productive, collaborative effort. When this is working, people contribute ideas, use their initiative and are open to change. They are interested in what they do, care about their customers or clients, and are eager to learn and grow.

To build this style of leadership you need to be aware of the sources of power at your disposal and use them to influence others in positive ways. Over time, you will extend your repertoire and capacity to influence by building your expertise, reputation, networks, communication skills, personal warmth, knowledge of company systems, and much more.

In the next chapter we will delve more deeply into the practicalities of being an inspiring leader. We will look at some of the factors that might frustrate your efforts to be everything you can be as a leader, as well as some suggestions about how to deal with them.

Chapter 4
People and relationships

In hiring a worker one always hires the whole man.
... one cannot 'hire a hand',
its owner always comes with it.

Peter Drucker

> *In this chapter ...*
>
> *You will learn about the characteristics of leaders and teams where high performance is sustained over the longer term. We will also look at some impediments to good teamwork, including historical factors and modern competitive pressures that can undermine trust and collaboration. Some suggestions for reducing the impact of these impediments are suggested towards the end of the chapter.*

The new productivity equation

If you ask anyone who has been in the workforce for a long time, they will tell you that work is more intense now than it has ever been. Employees are expected to fit more into the day, deadlines are shorter and there are more people to please. The reasons for this include more intense competition, tighter margins, customers who want more and the seemingly endless call for greater efficiencies.

Organisations across all sectors are affected. Senior management everywhere is demanding high performance outcomes that are sustainable over the longer term. This is a big ask. It is one thing to want exceptional results for a special or important project, but quite another to expect people to repeat the success (or do more with less) time after time. Think about it. If you are interested only in getting it right once, or over a short timeframe, you might be happy enough to push hard and leave some damage in your wake – wasted resources, exhausted staff and the like. But if you want people to turn up the next day willing and able to take on a new challenge, then you have to do it differently. Individually and as a team they need to be energised by the experience and ready to take on more.

What does it take for leaders to deliver sustainable high performance? We can express it through a set of relationships that we will call **the new productivity equation**.

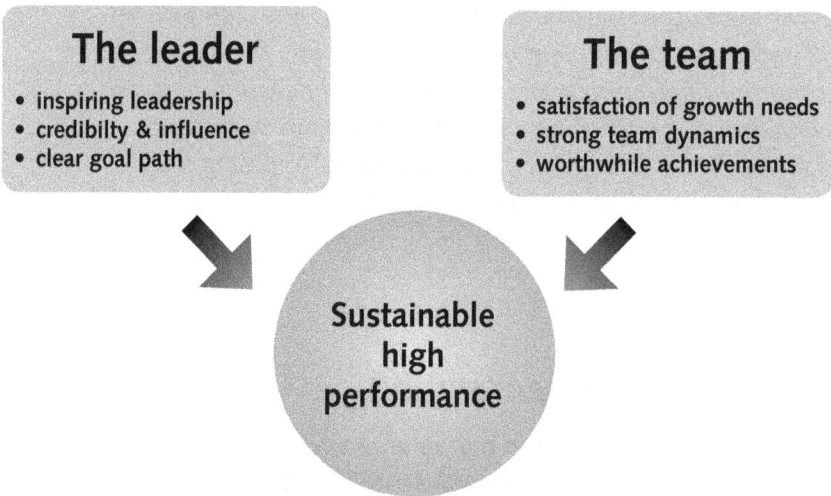

The leader
- inspiring leadership
- credibilty & influence
- clear goal path

The team
- satisfaction of growth needs
- strong team dynamics
- worthwhile achievements

Sustainable high performance

The role of the leader is crucial. As we saw in Chapter 3, inspiring leaders use an empowering style to engage people. They communicate high expectations because they believe that this form of encouragement brings out the best in people. They have credibility because they are seen as trustworthy and deliver on their promises, and they use their power and influence to grow the team's resources and capability.

Just as important, all of this is grounded in the reality that results have to be delivered. Therefore, effective leaders provide a clear path to team goals by making sure that everyone's role is clear and unambiguous, people know what they are accountable for, and work processes are streamlined and on target.

Results are delivered through team effort, so the best leaders make sure that the team is both willing and able to keep performing at a high level. The three most important team factors are noted in the new productivity equation. Individuals whose growth needs are met through their work and achievements are highly motivated. Achievements, when shared, feed into a strong team dynamic where people feel included, valued and in control of their work. This is the foundation for shared learning and a strong sense that the team's achievements make a difference to their customers or clients.

How can you tell when the new productivity equation is in play? You will see people doing the following:

- ✓ working with energy and purpose
- ✓ enjoying what they are doing
- ✓ appearing to be interested in what everyone around them is doing
- ✓ being willing to share their know-how and expertise, and be a sounding boards for others' ideas
- ✓ using their skill and initiative
- ✓ taking matters of work quality and customer satisfaction very seriously.

What else? If you meet them socially, they will tell you they like their jobs, their colleagues and the organisation they work for. (People are quick to run down their employer if they are dissatisfied with the way they are treated.)

The new productivity equation sets the bar very high. You might wonder if it is really necessary and what is driving it. If two reasons could be sifted out from all the others, they would be the rise of international competition and customer demand for better quality and service.

What difference has international competition made to organisations? Well, companies have to be very good at what they do to survive, and they have to do it cost effectively. If not, they are likely to lose out to competitors, go out of business or see their facilities or skills migrate offshore where costs are lower and local conditions are more favourable for business. That is why, over the past few decades, organisations have responded to fierce competition by streamlining operations and trying to ensure that every employee is focused and productive.

And customer demand? Yesterday, business was about manufacturing products and providing uniform services. They could succeed by mass-producing items of so-so quality. Today, success comes from responding to customer demand. Many employees are at, or close to, the customer interface. It is important that they know what customers want and are responsive to them. Tastes change quickly so companies have to be innovative to keep up. Disappointed customers can and do go to the competition. Many tell their friends, and they do it very efficiently through social media.

So organisations need employees who are close to the customer experience and want to meet their expectations. They need employees to think in terms of quality, adding value, and delivering as promised. This takes excellent leadership, teamwork and a genuine interest on the part of everyone in what they do. This would simply not be possible under a controlling or inflexible leadership style where initiative and creativity are stifled, the focus is on producing things rather satisfying customers, and people do only what they have to do to get by.

What is holding leaders back?

The attitudes of contemporary leaders are generally quite egalitarian. They believe that people do want to make a contribution and respond well to a supportive and encouraging work environment. We also noted that on the evidence from surveys many leaders appear to be falling short when it comes to putting their attitudes into action. As a result, the laissez-faire style of leadership is commonplace and the majority of employees are not as engaged in their work as they could be. The situation is far from ideal.

As a leader, you want to do better than the majority. Having read this far you already know about your role and what it takes to be an inspiring leader with credibility and a focus on team and organisational goals. You have already been introduced to all of the factors in the new productivity equation, and more will follow in later chapters. There is much to consider, but if you take a systematic approach you will become the leader that others look up to.

If anything is holding you back at this point, it is a lack of confidence in your ability to put the new productivity equation into practice. Do not let that stop you:

- ✓ Just make up your mind and take the first step.
- ✓ Get out of your office and connect with people.
- ✓ Show your belief in their ability by setting high expectations.
- ✓ Take the team into your confidence.
- ✓ Leave your ego at the door – no one expects you to have all the answers.
- ✓ Notice the energy in the room rise when everyone is involved and searching for solutions.
- ✓ Let team members take the credit for what all of you have done.

Other reasons why laissez-faire leadership is so prevalent are more to do with modern organisations and their history than the preferences or choices of individual leaders. In the following sections we will take a trip back into history, with a focus on how relationships between leaders and team members have changed over the past 100 years or so. You will see that relationships used to be strained and even hostile and it has not been easy to shake off this legacy.

Other impediments relate to modern business pressures and the drive for efficiencies that can strain relationships between people and their leaders. Sometimes leaders slip back into a directive style when they have to do more with less, or are obliged to make difficult changes, such as reduce staff numbers. In the final section we will discuss some ways for leaders to manage their way through these pressures.

The pull of history

Some impediments to good leadership can be put down to the pull of history. Douglas McGregor exposed the problem of entrenched Theory X attitudes and challenged the managers of his era by asking, 'What are your assumptions about the most effective way to manage people?' He knew the answer before he even posed the question. 'Keep an eye on people, watch out for any signs of laziness and punish anyone who breaks the rules.' He understood how damaging such attitudes were for forming productive working relationships. How could people give their best while being regarded by their managers as less than fully rounded adults who were incapable of taking responsibility and aspiring to bigger things?

But the problem did not stop there. McGregor saw that over time Theory X habits and mindsets had become embedded in policies and practices for managing every part of the organisation. Even worse, the very fact that they existed reinforced the idea they were necessary – the self-fulfilling prophecy of authoritarian attitudes.

An example of what McGregor meant was the ubiquitous time clock. This is how it worked. Typically, on arrival at work a person would pick up his or her attendance card, push it into a machine that registered the time with a loud ding or crunch, and then replace it on a stand. The process was repeated for meal breaks and at the end of the work day. The system prevented people from falsifying their attendance records and managers could dock their pay for arriving late – and they did.

You could say it was a fair system because everyone was treated the same. The problem was, of course, that clocking on and off was used because of an absence of trust in the honesty and reliability of workers and it did give people the sense that they were being herded into work like sheep. It was the epitome of Theory X thinking. Most time clocks have disappeared now and have been replaced with more subtle means of keeping time. Flexible work hours are relatively common too, and did not exist at all in McGregor's time. However, a clock-watching mindset is still evident in many workplaces. How much time do people at your workplace spend debating the merits of coming into the office as opposed to working from home or other locations, or the relative importance of time spent at work versus the amount of work completed or results achieved?

How are working hours managed in your organisation? What are the procedures and practices for keeping tabs on how much time people spend working? How far along the Theory X and Theory Y scale would you place yourself and your workplace on this issue?

Consider the HR policies, guidelines and practices used where you work. Are any features there simply to ensure people toe the line rather than be trusted to make sensible and reasonable decisions for themselves? Procedures for monitoring performance, granting leave, terminating contracts, and the rest, usually contain numerous clauses about entitlements, penalties and other provisions. Of course many of these are necessary – the absence of rules can be chaotic. But look closely and you will find that some are more of a burden than a help, more about controlling people than encouraging them, and more likely to promote mediocrity than excellence. Modern HR is far less controlling and draconian than it used to be. However, many changes have been made incrementally, without any major challenge to the underlying assumptions. A lot of Theory X thinking has slipped through as a result.

How comfortable are you about loosening the controls?

Take this test of Theory X and Theory Y for the 21st century. Try to respond with a simple 'yes' or 'no' to each statement:

- I am not very comfortable with people working from home or remotely.
- The bulk of the time in my team meetings is for telling people 'how it is' or for checking on their progress.
- People who want flexibility for work-life balance reasons lack commitment or ambition.
- People generally slacken off if I am not there to supervise them.
- I value the chance to use my initiative and develop my skills more than the people in my team.

If you answered 'yes' to one of these statements you might be inclined towards Theory X thinking in some situations. If you responded this way to two or more statements, then your attitudes could be too embedded in the past. Reflect on them, or compare your thoughts on matters like these with your peers.

Look anywhere in your organisation and you are likely to find mechanisms for checking, verifying and monitoring. Some of them have a sensible purpose, but others are simply excessive and just get in the way. If, as a leader, you sometimes feel you are caught in a time warp, you may be right.

Nowhere is this more apparent than in organisations that are very traditional, or have been around for a long time. Examples that come to mind include railways, hospitals, financial institutions, universities and local government organisations. In workplaces like these, ways of doing things are often entrenched in past practices, and change is harder to achieve. In the following scenario we meet Jeff, who is a physiotherapist in Margo's team at the hospital:

> *Sitting in the tea room, Jeff glanced at his phone and noted that he had only four minutes left of his break. Better get back to the treatment room in time or there would be trouble! For the third time that week he seriously questioned his decision to take a job at the hospital rather than joining the small physio practice where they had offered flexible work hours, a choice of areas to specialise, and the chance to progress if he worked hard. With a young family to support, Jeff had opted for the security of the big employer.*

> *He enjoyed the work but had not anticipated the amount of red tape that covered just about everything. The hours were inflexible and if he needed a day off he had to submit endless forms and go on hand and knee to his supervisor, Margo. He worried that his application for study leave would be rejected because 'he had not been there for long enough'. And it wasn't just about him. He knew of a new treatment that was getting excellent results elsewhere, but was not permitted to try it here because 'our established procedures have always provided good outcomes so there is no need to change anything'.*

Here we have Jeff's views about the difference between working in a traditional organisation and a small professional practice. It is easy to understand Jeff's frustration and his desire to be where he thinks the leadership would be more progressive. In reality, organisations are still evolving and some have a long way to go. Margo has inherited some rigid policies and procedures. Spending the bulk of her time on admin and paperwork is one of the reasons why she has less time to spend with her team and she is leaning towards the laissez-faire leadership style.

Well-oiled machines

To be fair, the Theory X approach to leadership delivered results for a very long time – it is how things were done for thousands of years. Historically, it built monuments and roads, marched armies, organised tax collections, ruled nations, managed monasteries, ran shipping lines and the like. As a way of organising vast numbers of largely uneducated workers, willing or conscripted, and working them for long hours on arduous tasks, it came up trumps. At times, no doubt, these workers would have shown enormous skill and commitment, but on the whole, getting the job done was about assembling people and materials and just keeping them at it.

This kind of leadership was still there at the start of the Industrial Revolution in Europe, a time when the bulk of economic activity shifted from small home-based farms and businesses to large industrial centres. But what kind of leadership did the industrialists use? The lessons of history were adapted to the new circumstances and in the 19th century world of factories and mass production, Theory X leadership found a new home.

Managers were needed in large numbers but there was no education in management science as we have today. They were generally chosen for their higher social status rather than education or ability and more or less made up the rules as they went along. On the other side were the workers, largely dispossessed farmers and artisans with little choice other than to seek a livelihood in the new production centres. This was not a good start for enlightened management practices or collaborative workplace relationships.

Eventually, Frederick Taylor[19], an industrial engineer known as the 'father' of Scientific Management, entered the scene. He was disturbed by what he saw – workplaces that were poorly run, disorganised and dangerous. He wanted to improve industrial efficiency and the work environment. Ultimately, Taylor laid the foundations of modern factory management – standardised procedures, operational controls, equipment design and precise training in work methods.

Did you know Taylor believed that relationships between managers and workers should be cooperative and based on respect? It is true, but in his mind the best way to achieve this was for managers to run the show with workers doing exactly as they were told. Managers would learn about the best scientific work methods, train the workers, and closely supervise them to ensure conformity. You could say that Taylor invented micromanagement. It wasn't that he had a dim view of the workers – he believed that they wanted to do their best, but they needed to be closely guided by their managers in the most efficient work methods. For Taylor, it was all about the science.

At about the same time, Henry Ford figured out how to make the entire system of production more efficient with a moving assembly line. Instead of having groups of workers putting a whole Model T together, the chassis went onto a conveyor where workers added a piston here and a door handle there as it passed by. Model Ts began to roll out of the factory in large numbers. The superiority of the assembly line method of production, combined with Taylor's job re-engineering methods, was beyond doubt. Well-oiled machines, indeed!

For Taylor and Ford things could not have been better! Ford was making money and paying exceptionally high wages for the time. Taylor believed that improved work methods would allow workers to optimise their output and expected that management would compensate them fairly for it – after all, payment was commonly linked to individual output in those days.

In the real world things were different. Taylor underestimated the greed of most factory owners (they were not paying big wages), and failed to anticipate other problems – conflict, sabotage, confrontations between unions and management, poor quality, lack of job fulfilment and absenteeism. All of these were symptoms that relationships between managers and the workers were at a very low ebb.

The problem of control and power

What was the problem? If one word sums it up it would have to be 'control'. Scientific Management was a system for finding the 'one best way' to do things, with managers firmly in charge and monitoring the workers closely to guarantee compliance. In the matter of personal autonomy and pride in their work, it was a case of workers nil, management one. The 'Pin Maker'[20] illustrates the situation that a typical artisan might have found himself in during that era.

With the benefit of hindsight we can easily see that jobs designed around the principles of Scientific Management left workers feeling deskilled, pressured and dehumanised. And with little power to protest openly, they used covert means like sabotage and strikes to make their feelings known. As McGregor ultimately realised, attitudes had hardened on both sides. Management came to believe that workers were lazy and needed to be pushed and prodded, recognisable to us as a Theory X mindset. Workers lost trust in their managers and limited output, fearing that a show of productive effort would simply result in pressure to continue to do more and more. The problem of Theory X had turned full circle.

By the 1950s (not so long ago) the roughest edges of Scientific Management had been chipped away. Working conditions were improving and the 'war' between management and workers was settling down. But in the main, jobs remained narrow and unfulfilling and management still called most of the shots. And it was not just about factories. If you have seen pictures of the typical 1960s or 1970s era administration unit, you will recall desks lined up in neat rows with the supervisor out front ever watchful for signs of idleness or worse, social chatter. It was a case of tail up, head down and do what you were told.

Given this background, it is little wonder that relationships between leaders and workers are sometimes strained. It has taken decades for attitudes to change on both sides, and for suspicion to be replaced by trust.

The Pin Maker

Imagine yourself as an artisan pin maker (like your dad and granddad before you) now forced to seek work in a pin-making factory. You arrive to find that the technicians have identified 18 separate steps in the pin-making process and have decreed that each worker will be employed on only one of these. It's more efficient this way, they explain. While a single artisan can make only x pins each day, using these modern methods the factory can produce xxx. Your job is to sharpen the pin points. You are given a special sharpening tool and told exactly how to use it. You need the money so you take the job.

At the end of the week you join the pay line, and are shocked and disappointed at the small amount in your pay packet! You protest that the factory has made thousands of pins during the week and must be making a huge profit! Perhaps so, reply the technicians, but you are just a worker doing a simple job that only required one hour of training. What more could you expect? You walk away confused and downcast.

You think about the good old days when you were your own boss. You made beautiful pins that were finely crafted with handmade tools. No one stood over you or checked your work a dozen times a day. You took a break when you needed it, chatted to people passing by, and knocked off at the end of the day when you were satisfied with the day's work. And you were never bored ... not like now!

Modern impediments to collaborative work relationships

The new productivity equation might seem to be more of an ideal state than a description of the reality that you have experienced. The relentless drive for greater efficiency, including large team sizes, sometimes makes it more difficult for leaders to maintain good relationships with their teams. You might recognise some of the modern day impediments to productive work relationships in the following paragraphs.

Happy workplaces

Some leaders do not understand the logic behind the new productivity equation, and see a congenial team atmosphere as an end in itself, rather than as the basis for achieving results. Here is a brief scenario to illustrate the point.

> *Carl breezed into Alex's office for his regular one-to-one with each team member. He had little time to divide among the 16 or so planners, but saw it as important to touch base on a personal level.*
>
> *'I appreciate the job you are doing, Alex, those applications for adjustments to the size of advertising billboards in the main street can be a real headache...' Alex started to ask about joining the town centre redevelopment project she had heard was coming up but trailed off when Carl started on about his stupid new SUV. What was the point anyway? Last time a new project came up he gave it to his friend Jon. Feeling deflated and a little cynical, she watched as Carl strode off to connect with the next happy camper on his list.*

Carl is naturally an outgoing person and likes being with the people in his team. He wants them to get on well together and to enjoy coming in to work. However, he is missing the mark and is coming across as shallow and out of tune with some people's needs and aspirations. To turn this around he should listen more carefully, connect team members with the right opportunities and help them to succeed. This would add substance to his leadership.

Leaders like Carl do benefit when people are happy for the right reason, and that is when they are performing well.

Team celebrations, laughter and smiles all round are good for team morale – they promote a can-do attitude and they help to build trust. Carl will do better when he understands the connection between productivity and a great team atmosphere, and that leadership is not just about spreading sunshine and good humour.

Scientific Management is still with us

Whether we like it or not, most organisations are built around the principles of Scientific Management, modified for our times. In some ways we do Scientific Management a lot better now. Competitive pressure and efficiency drives have led to refinements in planning, scheduling, procuring, staffing, programming, budgeting, performance managing, and so on. More than ever, organisations operate as well-oiled machines with people tied to their rhythms and requirements.

Although Theory X reminders like time clocks have largely disappeared and workplaces are more relaxed and congenial, bureaucratic rigidities are still widely in place – some necessary and others just plain irritating. The senior management penchant for personal and group performance data has never been greater and technology gives them ready access to it. While good managers use this information to make sure that all the systems are in balance, others use it as a tool for taking excessive control that ultimately stifles energy and creativity.

Good leaders are generous with their information. They use it to keep people informed about progress and results and to help them understand what is going on in the larger organisational context. When technology is used to monitor individual performance, leaders make the process transparent and are never caught out using the information in a covert way, or for purposes that are not clear to everyone.

No one is irreplaceable

For many people it is hard to get the kind of work they want, especially jobs that are secure or full-time. Increasingly, newly created jobs are part-time, or are available on a contract basis. Only people with skills or knowledge in short supply, or critical to the firm's core business are in a strong bargaining position. Most other people know that they are not indispensable, and if things turn bad, they can be out of a job all too quickly.

This situation creates problems for good leaders. It unsettles employees and makes it harder to establish a trusting relationship with them. How can they fully trust you when they fear being tossed aside if they don't measure up in your eyes? Even if they work hard, all it takes to threaten their position is a business downturn or a structural change. Can you really expect people to give 100% when they are worried about their futures?

Some leaders use situations like this to strengthen their power and control over team members. They use the threat of redundancy, veiled or otherwise, as a device to keep people on their toes. Certainly, people do knuckle under in these circumstances, but an atmosphere of fear undermines performance. It is far better to motivate people in positive ways.

As leader, you do not have a crystal ball and cannot make promises about secure employment or opportunities that might not eventuate. However, you can give people every opportunity to develop their capabilities so that they are competitive for other employment if they have to move on.

The drive for results

The environment in contemporary organisations is often quite pressured. As the leader you might receive the not-so-subtle message that you have to do more with less, or win more business in an increasingly competitive environment. You are left with the uncomfortable feeling that you are 'the meat in the sandwich'. You want to support your team but you are expected to be on side of management. So when under pressure to deliver you may feel you have to place extra demands on your team, or make compromises you would rather avoid. It is a real dilemma.

The difficult leadership balancing act

A pure form of leadership excellence is a little out of sync with the reality of most contemporary organisations. You want to give people the opportunities and flexibility that they need, but are under pressure to deliver results, unreasonable as they may be at times. Sometimes you have to turn down requests, or make unpopular decisions. Leaders often struggle to find the right balance.

In short, leadership these days requires endless concessions and compromises. It's a balancing act where you try your best to give your people what they need as individuals with complex needs and aspirations, and delivering the bottom-line results that your own boss expects. Here are some suggestions to help you succeed, even in difficult circumstances.

Keep building your team

'Working as a team' is used so often these days that it has become a cliché. But despite the rhetoric, teams often generate more frustration and conflict than genuine collaboration and joint problem solving. On the other hand, teams sometimes work brilliantly, so much so that it seems almost spontaneous. But look more closely and you will see careful planning behind the success. It is about clarity of purpose, good team structure and getting the team's social dynamics right. But most of all, team success is about leadership.

In Chapter 5 you will be introduced to some practical team-building ideas to start applying immediately. Even when the team is working well you need to stay vigilant because a high-functioning team can be easily upset by the unexpected, causing morale and performance to drop quickly. Imagine, for example, a situation where senior management is displeased with a team's results – perhaps output has fallen or customer satisfaction ratings are down – and the team leader is feeling the heat. She starts looking for flaws or mistakes. She looks around for the slothful, incompetent or reckless – the bad apples. She berates her team and demands better performance or else. People disperse with their collective tails between their legs.

Of course, an approach like this would be disastrous. Blaming and finding fault are short cuts to undermining trust. People respond by covering up problems, holding back their ideas, and retreating into their shells. And trust is very hard to win back once it has been lost.

What would have been a better response on the part of the leader? She would start by seeking answers to the performance problems in her own behaviour. She would ask herself what she had missed, how changes she introduced had unanticipated consequences on how well things worked, or if she had failed to explain something of importance to the team. An effective leader recognises the impact of their own behaviour on team performance.

Let's see how the situation played out when Carl was told by his manager that the time between the submission of commercial development applications and their sign-off by his team had increased by two weeks, and was now among the worst of any local government agency in the state. Carl is worried, and has asked Phil, his friend and mentor, to meet over coffee.

> 'I just can't believe it,' said Carl. 'I have only been in the job for three months. Why is she blaming me?'
>
> 'Well, someone has to take responsibility and you are in the hot seat,' replied Phil, as direct as ever.
>
> Carl stared into his coffee cup. 'I thought I was making a difference. I get on well with most of them and the atmosphere around the team has really picked up. I need to toughen up and insist that those files come through a lot faster.'
>
> 'Look,' said Phil, 'I have said this before – your people do not want you as a friend. They want a leader who brings out the best in them and appreciates their work. Give them a challenge – something to aim for. And while you are at it, stop making assumptions about the people who have been there a long time and spread the interesting jobs around. And don't try to play the tough guy. It just isn't you, and it wouldn't work anyway.'
>
> As he headed back to his office, Carl thought over the last thing that Phil said to him. 'See this as an opportunity.'

Hopefully, Carl will rethink his approach and get serious about building a team that can meet challenges like shorter timelines without compromising quality. For Carl and every leader like him, team building is a leadership task that needs constant work and attention.

Go in to bat for your team and grow your capacity to influence

If your own boss is more demanding than you think is reasonable, go in to bat for your team. There is nothing wrong with pushing back and making your views known. For instance, Margo's team of physiotherapists has had resources cut over recent years. There is no point in complaining because no one is listening. However, if she analyses the impact of these cuts and can articulate how more support would make a difference to patient outcomes, she has a reasonable chance of convincing Anthony. In fact, she has already argued successfully for that new piece of equipment. To capitalise on this success, she should evaluate its effectiveness after a suitable interval, and make sure that Anthony and those he answers to know about the difference it made. After that, attracting resources to her unit will be much easier.

Sometimes leaders find that changes are thrust upon them without warning. Reduce your chances of being surprised or ambushed from above by staying as close as possible to the thinking of your own manager and those more senior. If you are in the loop, you are more likely to know or anticipate changes in outlook or strategy. This gives you more time and opportunity to prepare your team for a change in tempo. If you find this kind of thing happening too often, look at how well you are networking outside the team and work on your influencing skills.

As your credibility and experience grow, you will develop many sources of influence. These will be there to tap into when you need to bolster your team's resources or to influence decisions in your team's favour.

Use situational leadership

Should you change or adjust your usual style of leadership behaviour for any reason, or is there one approach that is generally the best? The short answer to the first part of this question is 'yes'. You do need to be watchful and responsive to the circumstances and adjust your behaviour accordingly because things rarely stay the same for long. That might mean being more directive than usual when a deadline has been moved forward, or supervising more closely when it is important that everyone works in unison to complete a complex project or assignment.

You do this already with team members who are less experienced or skilled. They take up more of your time and you tend to supervise them more closely. Giving more attention to less experienced or skilled people is not showing favouritism, nor is it over-controlling – it is simply being responsive to individual needs. Read the comments from real leaders showing how they respond to changing circumstances or people with different needs.

How real leaders respond to different people and events

I strive to be the person they need me to be at that point in time. Sometimes they need to me to be the cheerleader urging them to do their best; other times they need me to be the support person sitting quietly in their corner just trusting they can do it themselves. ~ Tracey Stewart

I strive to understand the significance of change and how the team can adapt to create opportunity. ~ David Akister

I strive to be the most appropriate leader for the particular situation – being a mentor or 'sounding board' on some occasions, and at other times taking decisive action. People respond to leadership in different ways: some resent advice and only require broad direction, while others crave feedback. So knowing your people is vital for being a good leader. ~ Alan Burgess

I try to gauge and understand the personalities and emotions of the people I lead and help them develop into a team that can adapt readily to change. I need to be flexible and change my management style to suit. Sometimes it is a case of the old saying – you have to treat people differently to treat them the same. ~ Scott Petrey

The central point is this – there is no single best way to lead in all situations. Leaders need a wide repertoire of skills and the flexibility to apply them as the need arises. As the leader, it is up to you to read the situation and provide the most appropriate kind of support that your team requires.

Over-communicate

Things can change very quickly in modern organisations. Sometimes you need to be more directive than usual, or you need to make quick or unpopular decisions without consulting the team. They may not like it. Some might be tempted to think or say that you are inconsistent or flaky.

So if you need to push your team harder than usual, talk openly about it. When things have settled back to normal, show appreciation for their efforts and let them air their feelings or grievances about the whole episode. A good debrief is a great tonic and will clear the air, especially over matters that were particularly difficult or poorly managed. A socially cohesive team will want to work it through so that they can do better next time.

How else can you handle these situations? Well, the first and best strategy is always to communicate with your team about what is going on. Over-communicate. Sometimes people need to hear the news more than once for it to sink in. It is reassuring to have unexpected things repeated. If they know why you are behaving a little differently or demanding more of them, they will usually be happy to fall in behind and do their bit. On the other hand, if you fail to explain the changes, they may simply feel put upon.

Time and again surveys have revealed that managers do not communicate as effectively as they think they do. When asked how comprehensive they are in explaining things to their staff, most managers will tell you that they do a great job most of the time. When the employees of these same managers are asked for their perspective, they consistently rate their managers quite poorly. Typically, employees think that managers are holding too much back. So take note, and be very deliberate in communicating your key messages.

Over to you

Contemporary leaders are under more pressure to deliver productivity gains than ever before. But sometimes, past history and modern pressures seem to conspire against them. More than ever before, leadership is a balancing act. On the plus side, most workplaces are now pleasant and safe and senior management is enlightened about a number of things that make coming to work desirable and rewarding.

Part of your ability to perform well in the leadership role relates to how well informed you are about people and their behaviour at work. The following chapters will provide that deeper knowledge of people and group dynamics, which is your foundation for guiding, motivating and developing your team. It will take you beyond the overused and superficial 'carrot and stick' approach to management, and encourage you to see your co-workers as fully rounded adults, just as you, yourself, are. As you build your skills in this area, you will find that exerting your influence is easier to do. Listening to you and pitching in will come more easily to team members and there will be less of the passivity and resistance that used to make coming to work a chore.

Chapter 5
Focus individual and team effort

To the person who does not know
where he wants to go
there is no favourable wind.

Seneca

In this chapter ...

You will find detailed suggestions for implementing strategies for focusing individual and team effort so that the work of your team is aligned with strategic organisational priorities. This covers the first of the three domains (recommended in this book) where you should develop your knowledge and capabilities to fully establish yourself as a leader.

People and strategy

Your team's goals and priorities should reflect the strategy of the organisation where you work. For your team to contribute relevant and worthwhile outcomes you need to know where your team fits into the larger picture. When you communicate a strong intent or purpose, people can focus.

In companies where corporate strategy and people management are closely linked there is generally a high performance culture, workforce stability, business sustainability, customer loyalty, employee satisfaction and strong revenues. All of this is, of course, planned when formulating HR strategy, in executing it, and in measuring the results. It doesn't happen by accident.

A clear vision or purpose needs to be sustained through planning and action. As team leader you can approach this in several ways. We will consider three in this chapter:

Clarifying roles and responsibilities: ensuring that every team member understands his or her role, and that there is a balance of roles and responsibilities across the team.

Managing individual work performance: giving regular feedback and using the company's formal performance appraisal system to link individual and team goals to the overall goals of the organisation.

Managing poor performers: actively assisting those at the tail end to lift their game.

Clarifying roles and responsibilities

In building a house, you would make sure that the foundations are solid. It is the same when building a team. The foundations of a house are bricks and mortar, for a team they are roles and responsibilities. It is all too easy to assume that everyone is clear about what is expected of them and that roles across the team are complementary. But if they are not, expect cracks to appear, conflicts to start and a loss of productivity and poor team morale to result.

Focused people

Everyone needs clarity around their contribution to the team effort. They need to:

- ✓ know what to do and what the priorities are
- ✓ understand what customers want
- ✓ appreciate when projects need to be completed and why
- ✓ understand how their work impacts on that of their teammates.

There is little point in leading good people only to see them spend too much time on the things that don't matter, or things that mattered yesterday but don't anymore. People resent being told that they were wasting their time after putting in a lot of effort – it dampens morale and undermines your credibility as a leader.

As the team leader, have you ever had thoughts that start with: You'd think they'd know ... and continue with things like ... how to do a spell check! ... to fill up with petrol when the tank gets low! ... to jump to attention when the big spenders turn up? If you find yourself fuming and muttering like this more often than you would like, try spending more time with people explaining the whys and wherefores. Effective performance in any role is governed by subtleties and unspoken rules that are easily misinterpreted. Team members are less likely to slip up if they have a more complete understanding of their role and your expectations.

Allocating a role means more than just listing out responsibilities or pointing to a job description. This will, at best, be sketchy and a bit out of date. There are always omissions, grey areas and uncertainties. As leader you need to check back frequently so that everyone is sure about what they are meant to be doing. Make it easy for them to make sensible and measured decisions about organising their work day and getting on with it.

Consider this scenario:

> Marilyn pulled in at the hospital's service entrance after a busy morning of picking up tissue and blood samples from the various labs around the suburbs. She was unprepared for the furious looks on the faces of the two technicians who greeted her. Where had she been? Why wasn't she back here an hour ago? They grabbed the canisters and quickly disappeared inside. Marilyn was upset and totally perplexed. She knew she was in for it but had no idea why.

Anything could have gone wrong here. Let us assume that Marilyn has considerable experience as a courier but is new to the health sector. Her new boss was confident in her capacity to perform the role but had not realised that the 'rules' were very different where she had worked previously. Her boss has failed to provide adequate briefings and, as a result, Marilyn was unaware that collections from a particular lab are always urgent, or that she should not stop for a lunch break while carrying samples due to the potential for spoilage.

This is a common situation. Managers frequently assume that people know what is expected or that the job requirements are so obvious that no explanation is needed. However, even the most straightforward job has its foibles and the potential to get something wrong is always there, especially for those who are new to the team. Consider, for example, safety requirements in your workplace – you have your rules and ways of doing things, but similar matters may be handled differently in other places. So as the leader it is safer for you not assume anything. Take the time to advise, listen, observe and answer questions. You may be surprised at how many things you thought were clear are, in fact, not. Here are a few pointers to put into practice:

- ✓ No job is simple, straightforward or requiring no explanation.
- ✓ Talk to each person about their role, responsibilities, and priorities.
- ✓ Your expectations might be different from those of their previous manager, so explain what they are.
- ✓ When you give an instruction, ask the person to explain it back to you to be sure you are both on the same page.
- ✓ Be very clear about timeframes and explain why they are important.
- ✓ If there is conflict between team members, a likely reason is that role boundaries or accountabilities are open to interpretation.
- ✓ Be the kind of leader to whom people will come if they are unsure.

Focused teams

The best teams understand what they are trying to achieve and have a clear sense of the priorities. Everyone has their role to play and the team dynamic revolves around collaboration. Putting the fundamentals of good team structure into place is critical to success – goals and priorities, standards, responsibilities and communication.

When goals and priorities are fuzzy, or people are unsure of their role in the team, things start to fall apart. Team morale drops because what they produce is not appreciated by management to the extent expected. There is confusion about who should be doing what and mumblings about poor communication and lack of support. Across team roles there is duplication on the one hand and things being overlooked on the other.

Look at the way that work flows within your team and between your team and others in the organisation. Teams can take on many different shapes, depending on the nature of the work undertaken. This affects communication and the amount of coordination needed to keep things on track. When people work closely together and timeframes for getting the job done are tight, then good communication and coordination are critical. Think about a flight crew landing an aircraft, a team of firefighters battling a bush fire, or medical professionals in an emergency room. Their roles are complementary and they have to work in sync with one another. There is no room for confusion or misunderstandings and someone is always firmly in charge.

Then there are teams where everyone contributes something unique but with less urgency so things can be more relaxed. Think of a team of marketing professionals working on an advertising campaign, a group of people working in sequence to make pizzas or students completing a group project. The most likely problem is that bottlenecks will form if someone slips behind or cannot deliver as expected. This tends to happen when roles or accountabilities are poorly delineated or timeframes and expectations about standards are unclear.

The team with the least need for close communication and coordination is one where roles have little overlap because people are mostly independent of one another and results are pooled only at the end of the reporting period. People come together for team meetings and get-togethers but do not depend on one another on a daily basis. Think of a team of sales representatives with distinct sales territories or teachers with their allocation of classes. A key issue for coordination is that everyone works within agreed parameters including standards, timeframes and budgets. The most likely headache for leaders is that someone will be out of step and damage the reputation of the team.

The workflow pattern is quite static in some teams but for other teams it can change markedly with the situation. Firefighters, for example, spend considerable time at the fire station waiting to be called. They keep busy with maintenance, training and administration but do not need the same degree of coordination as they do when attending a fire. Teachers, on the other hand, work independently for most of the time. But even teachers work closely together sometimes, for example when completing student report forms or taking students on an excursion.

Margo's team of physiotherapists usually work one-to-one with clients and have a fairly regularised case load. But sometimes, with urgent or complex cases, they work in groups of two or three and need to coordinate closely. In addition, some of the children they treat are regular visitors to the hospital, requiring the physiotherapists to participate in multidisciplinary teams of health professionals. After starting in the team leader role, Margo quickly found that the administrative work involved in keeping track of the various cases and workload was quite onerous.

Carl leads a team of town planners, reviewing commercial development applications at the administrative centre of a large local government organisation. Generally, people work on their own but the bigger projects are delegated to the most experienced members of the team, who allocate some of the work to more junior colleagues. Coordination is not a big issue for him, or it shouldn't be. He has two problems – he does not have confidence in the skills of some of the senior planners to handle the more complex applications and some people grumble about who gets the best projects. He would like to please everyone but thinks it is out of the question.

Frank's team in the supermarket does a range of things – unloads delivery vehicles, manages the storerooms, checks on stock levels in the storerooms, restocks the shelves in the supermarket, and keeps all areas hygienically clean and tidy. Only the few who work in the small delicatessen are at all specialised. Frank likes to stay close to the action and allocates people to jobs as they come up, making sure they do them to the correct standards.

The work is mostly routine, except when a truck comes in late or there is an unexpected run on particular food items. He enjoys the buzz as people busy themselves sorting things out but he wonders if things could be more organised.

As you can see, coordinating the work of other people is not easy, even when team members work fairly independently, as is the case with Carl's group. Even choosing to whom tasks and projects should be allocated can be problematic. And regardless of the kind of team you lead there will be times when you have to step in and take control and other times when you sit down with everyone and organise the work together. The best leaders are flexible – they are responsive to the situation and can shift between the two. You need to understand the way the work flows within and around your team, and be capable of fostering collaboration. Tools to help with each of these leadership tasks follow.

Role and responsibility charting

A tool often used to map work flows is known as **role and responsibility charting**. There is not enough room here to describe the full process but you can adapt the main ideas quite easily.

Basically, you identify the key outcomes for which your team is responsible and map the steps in the process for achieving those outcomes. As you do so, you identify the person(s) responsible for each step and the people with whom they need to communicate to keep the work flowing smoothly. Repeat the process for each key outcome.

Use the diagnostic questions in the chart over the page to guide your thinking. You can also use these questions as discussion starters with your team.

Role and responsibility charting tool

Elements to chart	Diagnostic questions	Points to consider
Key deliverable or outcome	What is your team expected to contribute? What standards are expected?	Consult your own manager; refer to the strategic or operational plan.
Steps in work process	What are the steps or stages? What is the value add at each step? Are there any bottlenecks in the process?	Expect at least one process per key deliverable or outcome. Check for missed or unnecessary steps. Check for confusion about purpose, or wastage of time/resources.
Responsibilities	Who in the team is involved at each step? Who is accountable for results? Does accountability rest at the appropriate level? Are there any gaps or overlaps across roles that disrupt the work process?	If more than one person is involved, note who is accountable for the overall effort. Check for lack of role clarity. Check for signs of conflict or blaming that might be caused by gaps & overlaps.

Relevant others	Who needs to be consulted over progress or changes? Who needs to be kept informed?	Identify people within your team, as well as those outside, who are affected by your work processes.
Support	What support (skills, materials, training, etc.) is needed to support the process? How do you as leader provide support?	Check the inputs & resources needed to support performance. Consider your leadership role in supporting each work process.
Downstream & upstream	Who is involved in the work process before it reaches your team? What are the next stages for your team's deliverables or outcomes?	Identify the people who channel work to or provide inputs for your team. Check on what happens next. Consider how well you & your team are communicating with people upstream & downstream.

You can use **role and responsibility charting** in a number of ways. Used as a desk exercise for yourself only, it will quickly let you know how well informed you are and provide insight into the issues that you need to clarify or follow up. You could also use it to focus team discussions around productivity or other relevant issues. For instance, conflicts are often caused by lack of role clarity or confusion between people about who has responsibility (and not personalities, as is often assumed).

Another way to look at **role and responsibility charting** is through the three central themes of people, process and resources. This is depicted in the following diagram:

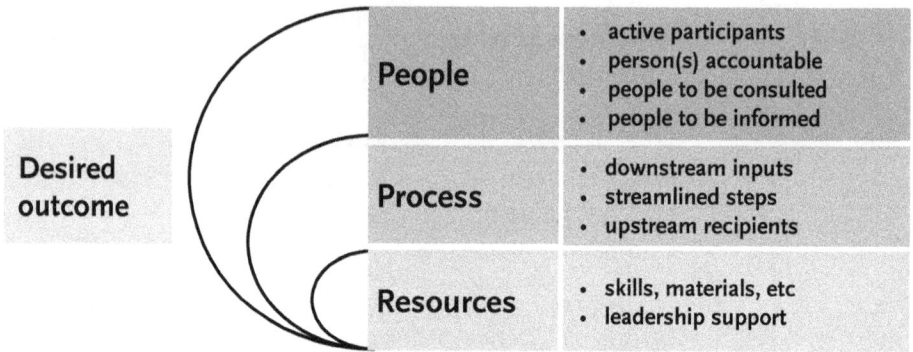

	People	• active participants • person(s) accountable • people to be consulted • people to be informed
Desired outcome	**Process**	• downstream inputs • streamlined steps • upstream recipients
	Resources	• skills, materials, etc • leadership support

If you are involving the team, plan how you will lead the discussions. Ask for input and use brainstorming or other techniques to give everyone a say. Even if you have real concerns about how your team is performing, focus discussions on the positives – what is working (rather than what is not). Why? Because people are energised and more likely to engage when invited to revisit the successes and more than happy to suggest ways to improve. Dwell on the failures and they will switch off and become defensive. 'How can we do better?' is far preferable to asking 'What are we doing badly?'

Let's catch up with Frank who is holding a team meeting to discuss responsibilities and standards. It is a quiet time in the supermarket, and Kaitlin has supplied temporary staff, so most of the team are present. She has coached Frank on how to conduct the meeting and he has agreed to give her ideas a go.

'As you all know,' began Frank, 'last Wednesday we had two serious customer complaints – one that under the top layer of strawberries, the punnet was a gooey mess and the other about a frozen meal being almost at room temperature. This isn't good enough.' Frank noticed the frosty looks around the room and bit his tongue before going on. 'We can do better. That is why we welcome customer feedback and why we are here today. I want to hear your ideas about how we can make sure problems

like these remain in the past.'

Jill was the only one looking his way. 'The trouble is, half the time the delivery trucks come in late or all at the same time. There are not enough people around to get things out and stacked, the stores out back get filled to overflowing, and there is a panic to get the stuff onto the supermarket shelves or into the fridges. That's what happened last Wednesday – we had to pile the frozen meals up and that's why some got defrosted. There you have it!'

Frank took a moment to recover himself. He had to think quickly, before others had a chance to follow with complaints and more stories of defeat. 'Thanks, Jill. You have given us some specific areas to work on. We were tripped up last Wednesday by those deliveries. I would like us to be clearer about the food handling procedures from the dock to the store and make sure that we can manage it better, even when something unexpected happens. How about we spend some time mapping it out, and seeing where we can do better?' Frank was relieved to see heads starting to nod in agreement.

'And could you find out why those delivery trucks are not arriving on schedule, or if they can let us know if they are running late?' asked Jill.

The meeting is off to a good start. Frank wanted to lecture to the team but caught himself just in time. For the first time, he is seeing problems like over-stacked fridges as systemic and not simply as due to the negligence of individual team members. It is a new way of looking at things. He is also realising that, to really understand how to improve food handling standards, he will need to listen and consult with the team far more than he has done in the weeks since he started in his new role. And with people like Jill in the team, he knows he will be held accountable!

Role and responsibility charting is ideal for any leader in a situation similar to the one that Frank finds himself in. It points to the main considerations when tracking a work process and provides a structure for working them through. Leaders can also use it to reinforce important behaviours or attitudes without having to single out individuals who might have fallen short (with regard to certain food handling standards in Frank's case).

Team dynamics and work quality

Mike Blansfield and Marvin Weisbord[21], two widely-respected organisation development consultants, focused on how to get better quality results. They identified three aspects of the team's dynamics that influence the quality of the team's work and and what could be changed to achieve better outcomes. The three factors are a sense of belonging or being a part of the group, a feeling of control over one's involvement in the team, and being valued for skills. Over many years of observation during the 1970s and 1980s the consultants found that when these three factors were switched on for team members, improvements in systems, processes, performance outcomes, trust and motivation followed.

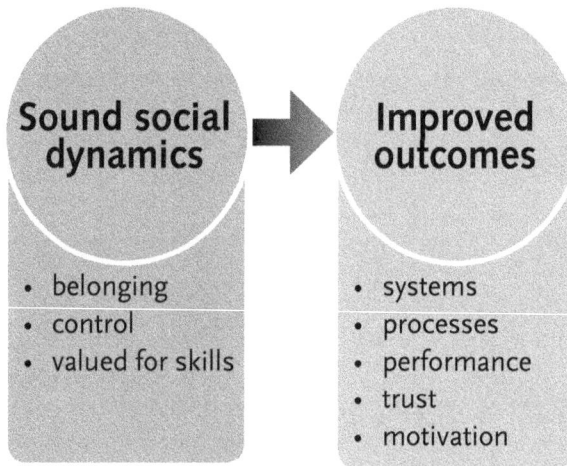

Sound social dynamics → Improved outcomes

- belonging
- control
- valued for skills

- systems
- processes
- performance
- trust
- motivation

As a new leader, one of the most significant things you can do is to embed these three factors into all of your team-building efforts. This is your key to creating a team of fully engaged people and being an inspiring leader. There are other things you want to do, of course, like clarify roles and responsibilities, decide how to share decision making and set up reward systems. However, these will be fully effective only if the social dynamics of the team are all they could be.

The team dynamics checklist describes each of the three factors and suggests what a typical team member would feel and experience if that element is there for them. As leader, you can work through the three factors with every person you manage. You should find that the team is engaged and productive when everyone is okay on these issues.

Team dynamics checklist

Factor	Description	Team member feelings & experiences
Belonging	**Am I in or out?** When people feel valued & recognised as an insider, they collaborate.	I might not be in the front line, but my contribution is essential so I am equal to anyone else in the team. My idea did not get up but at least the boss listened & told me why we would not be doing the job that way – it made sense.
Control	**Do I have any power & control?** People want to understand their situation, to have choices & know what the future holds.	I am kept informed about what is happening in this organisation & changes in the pipeline. Along with the rest of the team I am consulted over the best methods. I am able to make decisions about how to complete my work.
Valued for skills	**Am I appreciated for what I have to offer?** People want to be recognised for their skill, experience & common sense, & not be dismissed because of misplaced assumptions & stereotypes.	I contribute something unique. My input helps the team succeed. People come to me for advice. My ideas are not overlooked because my position is low in the pecking order or I am new to the team.

You might be interested to know that since Blansfield and Weisbord drew on their practical experience to come up with this checklist, the latest thinking from neuropsychology has confirmed how relevant the team factors are. Knowledge gleaned from practical experience is sometimes supported by more rigorous research later on. In 1990, Seymour Epstein[22] identified four basic human needs as being to:

- feel attachment with other people
- understand the world around us, to know what the future holds and to feel in control
- protect and enhance our feelings of self-esteem
- maximise pleasure and avoid distress.

You will notice that the first three of these needs match each of the team effectiveness factors. The fourth one is implicit in Blansfield and Weisbord's approach – they assume that need satisfaction is important and achievements are motivating.

In 2007, Klaus Grawe, a psychologist, showed that Epstein's four needs are deeply ingrained in the wiring of the human brain. He came to two important conclusions[23]:

- When Epstein's four needs are met in social situations, people feel positive, optimistic and excited about the future. They are more open, inclusive, creative and resilient in the face of difficulties and setbacks.
- When these needs are compromised, people feel threatened, suspicious, stressed and anxious. They do less, and either withdraw from others or behave disruptively.

So, we now know that the elements identified by Blansfield and Weisbord are aligned with basic social needs that are powerful motivators. The neuropsychology supports their finding of superior team outcomes when these needs are fulfilled in a positive way. We can conclude that a sense of belonging, feeling in control and being valued for skills are potentially strong drivers of collaborative team behaviours. We can also predict that their absence will result in a lack of engagement and therefore detract from team performance. Here are some things you can do to create a positive social dynamic within your team:

- ✓ Acknowledge and value the contributions that each person makes.
- ✓ Create a climate and process for joint problem solving.
- ✓ Celebrate hard work, milestones and successes as a team.
- ✓ Ensure that everyone is treated fairly and with respect.
- ✓ Give people options and encourage them to take ownership.
- ✓ Explain current or future changes and why they are necessary.
- ✓ Draw on the skills within the team for new projects.

Let's catch up with Margo at an important team meeting. Anthony has come good on the promise of specialised physiotherapy equipment and she has just passed on the news.

'The approval has come directly from the executive team. They want me to pass on their congratulations for your great work, and the excellent patient recovery outcomes we have achieved.' There were smiles all around and Margo waited until the chatter died down. She continued. 'So it's in the pipeline, and we have time to set things up. We have a lot to think about – who will take the lead, preparing a treatment room, organising the training, and rearranging some of the case load.'

'Won't you just make all the arrangements and send an email around?' asked Jeff, surprised.

'Not this time. I have been here long enough to see how much skill and experience we have in this room. Besides, the hospital is implementing new patient management software – we could customise that to manage the caseload and track our patients more effectively so that we have more time actually providing the therapy. I think we should work together and make this happen as a team. We will get a better result that way.'

Jeff left the meeting feeling much better – his job was about to get a lot more interesting.

Without doing anything particularly hard or unusual, Margo has begun steering her team in a new direction by building the team's social fabric and involving them in the planning. This will lift the level of engagement and ultimately the team's capacity to do even better.

Managing individual work performance

Every organisation needs a sound platform for sustainability and growth. Most organisations of any size use a cyclical strategic planning process to work through their options. Typically this is based on 'management by objectives' (MBO), where the organisation's mission and goals are set out for the whole organisation and then cascaded down through each level. Ultimately, every group and individual has a performance plan that sits within the larger one, pointing to the contribution they are expected to make. Think of the overall plan as a mosaic, with each person represented by one tile.

Depending on your level of seniority, you may have taken part in a strategic planning process. For example, you might have developed an operational plan for your department, provided input to the company's strategic plan from your area of expertise, or sat around a table working up some goals and performance indicators with your team. If so, you will be well aware of how individual performance appraisal is linked to the organisation's overall performance planning process.

While MBO makes excellent sense, it is far easier to produce a strategic plan than it is to action it. The most obvious problem is that the world keeps changing and nothing stays static for long. A strategic plan is a bit out of date from the moment the ink is dry. It might look solid and reassuring with its mission statement, goals, key performance indicators and the like, but as Jack Welch[24] pointed out, you cannot reduce strategy to a formula. There is always the ebb and flow of economic activity, chance events, new discoveries and shifts in customer sentiment. The plan provides a useful starting point, but many features will change sooner or later.

The message for you as a leader is to prepare for the inevitable changes in priorities and timeframes, so:

✓ Stay close to the thinking within the top leadership team to understand how the priorities might be shifting.

✓ Review team plans frequently.

✓ Advise your team about shifts that affect their work.

✓ Keep them thoroughly briefed about where their roles fit in terms of the larger company direction.

Individual performance appraisal

A performance appraisal system (sometimes referred to as individual performance management) is the link between the organisation's strategic plan and the role assigned to each individual. It works like this. As the team leader you first sit down with your own manager and nut out the results for which you and your team will be accountable. Your own performance plan will specify goals, performance indicators, timeframes, and other details pertaining to your performance over the coming year. You then have a similar conversation with each person in your team, ensuring that they commit to their own set of outcomes.

Implementing a performance appraisal system is far from easy. It does take time to do it properly and the conversations with team members can be difficult. Managers commonly decry performance appraisal as a waste of time and energy. It is an even bigger waste of time to join the chorus. Think of it as a necessary evil if you must but make sure you know how the system works in your organisation and use it constructively to guide your team to better personal and collective achievements. It can be done well, although you are likely to be working with a system that is far from perfect. You can find ways to reduce the pain and increase the value.

Performance appraisal: understanding the pitfalls

Take note of the potential pitfalls and plan an implementation strategy so that these have a minimal effect on the value you and your team get out of the system.

There is not enough support from the top leaders

Leadership support is the most important ingredient in making anything work in organisations, especially something that is new or different. When it comes to performance appraisal, lack of leadership support really shows because everyone from the top down is expected to participate. When the senior leaders deride the system, spend only the minimal amount of time discussing performance ratings with their staff, or treat it as nothing more than a paper and pencil exercise, everyone gets the message that performance appraisal is just a distraction from the real business of managing. So do not be caught doing the same thing in front of your team.

It is treated as a discrete yearly event rather than as a continuous process

A key to getting performance appraisal right is to treat is as a cyclical process that begins with a discussion of plans for the coming year and ends with an assessment of performance outcomes. The leader meets regularly with the staff member to review progress and consider their support needs, indicating genuine interest in their development. Better still, there are no nasty surprises at the end of the year when performance ratings are given.

What sometimes happens, though, is that the leader does not follow up with the employee after the initial interview and nothing more is said until assessment time. Then, if views about performance ratings differ, both parties end up with hurt feelings that include confusion, disappointment and anger. In these situations you could say that the whole exercise was worse than useless.

There are too many goals or some goals are in conflict

Some of the confusion about performance appraisal occurs because the organisation is trying to do too much with it. Here are lists of the administrative and developmental purposes commonly specified in a performance appraisal policy.

Administrative purposes

- setting performance goals and targets
- monitoring and managing performance
- making decisions about pay rises

- making decisions about employee promotions
- collecting information for workforce planning.

Employee development purposes

- improving performance by providing coaching and feedback
- determining training needs
- exploring opportunities for growth and learning
- planning for career progression.

As you can see, there is a wide choice. Unless the actual purpose is made very clear, people form different understandings of what the system is for. They may even invent a purpose, such as 'a tool for management to decide who will be made redundant'. As you can imagine, it is all downhill from there.

It can also be hard for managers to balance the various expectations that are placed on them. For example, how do you get a team member to talk openly about their skill deficits when they think this might jeopardise their pay rise? How do you talk to a person about their training needs when you know there is no money in the budget to follow through?

Managers do not prepare properly for the performance appraisal interview

Managers sometimes complain that they do not have enough time to follow the whole company procedure, especially those with large teams, so do only as much as they have to do to satisfy basic requirements. They focus only on the paperwork – the administrative forms used in their organisation.

In response to this, you have to ask what leaders are for, and what is more important than one-on-one discussions about work plans and professional development. As is often the case, leaders can do more when they are organised and prepared.

Managers are not confident in giving feedback, either positive or negative

Lack of confidence, skill or training in speaking plainly with others is not confined to performance appraisal situations but it shows up strongly in this context. Think of a recent situation where someone paid you a compliment. How did you react? A little awkward or embarrassed? It is even harder to be the one giving the compliment! Now, think of a time when you had to speak to someone about a problem with their work or attitude. Having to raise problems is even harder than providing good feedback!

Giving feedback, positive or negative, is easier when it is done at the time, with little or no delay after the event that merited it. It can be really awkward when weeks or months have gone by. This is a good reason for having regular conversations with team members and not making them an infrequent or yearly event.

Making performance appraisal work

You can see why some managers do not look forward to performance appraisal (PA) time – it is one of the more difficult tasks on their busy agendas. Being prepared and organised makes all the difference. Here are some ideas to help you make it a success with your team.

Be prepared

- Know the purpose of PA in your organisation.
- Flow chart the steps in the process. (Remember it is cyclical!)
- Have the forms handy and know what information is required.
- Plan for a meeting with each member of your team.
- Review their previous PA documents and notes taken during the year.
- Give the person notice of the meeting and ask them to prepare.
- Take time to review your own assessment of their performance.
- Note down specific examples of their performance over the whole year, not just during recent weeks or months.
- Put the time aside for the meeting in a private location.

During the meeting

- Listen, ask for explanations, consider the person's views.
- Adopt a balanced approach to positive and negative aspects of performance.
- Compare their ratings (if used) with yours; discuss differences.
- Make performance plans for the year collaboratively.

- Agree on the year's training and development and be prepared to follow through.

After the meeting

- Make copies of signed documents and agreements.
- During the year have follow-up meetings with the person at least once per month.

If the performance appraisal system in your organisation is reasonably sound (it is fair and generally well accepted) you should manage your role well as long as you are organised. One of the hardest parts is holding conversations with people who disagree with your assessment of their performance. It is almost inevitable that this will happen sometimes. It is natural for us to recall the things we did well most vividly and to attribute our failures to unexpected changes, lack of support, too few resources and the like. Even so, everyone deserves a fair hearing, so listen hard because they might have a valid point. But in the end, it is up to you to make the assessment and to back it up with evidence. Most people are happy to accept a decision when it is explained to them. If you have communicated with them frequently during the year and have made diary entries and notes, you should be able to do this with relative ease.

Here is a glimpse of how it might go if you are well prepared:

Although he had been in the job for just four months, Carl was told by his manager that he was to complete performance appraisal interviews with everyone in his team. He had spoken to Alex the week before about the meeting, telling her what it was about and asking her to prepare. He, himself, had gathered the documents he needed. These included the department's performance appraisal guidelines, Alex's role description, her evaluation forms from the previous year and some notes he had made about her work.

A few minutes into the discussion, Carl moved to the subject of Alex's performance. 'As you know, Alex, I was not here earlier in the year, but I do have your performance assessments from last time. Overall, your previous manager rated you as a solid performer who had been with the department for 15 years. He made some notes before he left, mentioning that the number of development applications you assessed had slipped below the average group result. This tallies with my observations after I arrived. I know you have picked up lately but I would like to hear what you have to say about your work over the full year.'

Alex spoke for several minutes, surprised that Carl was actually listening.

'Okay, Alex,' he said, 'thanks for being open with me. So as you see it, you were doing everything expected of you and the notion that development applications had to be assessed within a certain timeframe is a recent thing, and was not properly explained to you. You had been promised some more interesting work but you feel as though you were overlooked more than once.'

'Yes, that about sums it up,' replied Alex. 'I have been here a long time but am still doing mostly routine files, despite the fact that my qualifications are better than some of the others. Things have been better lately because we are working more like a team, but I would really like more of a challenge.' She quietly reflected on the boredom she often felt and the day she almost threw an armful of files down the lift well in frustration. She thought it wise not to mention it.

'Well, Alex,' continued Carl a little later in the meeting, 'I can only give you an average performance rating this year. Although you have worked more efficiently of late, I have to take your performance over the whole year into account. But about the year ahead – would you like to join the team working on the town centre redevelopment project? It will be quite a challenge, but that is what you want, and with your experience and qualifications, you have a lot to offer.'

Why did this meeting go well, despite the fact that Carl had not been Alex's manager for the whole year (as often happens due to frequent staff movements in many organisations)? Both prepared for the meeting, Carl invited Alex to open up and listened. He took her performance over the whole year into account and he responded to her requests for some changes in her responsibilities.

Managing poor performers

Most people start a job with good intentions. They want to enjoy their tasks and contribute something back. But in some cases things go awry and their performance slips below an acceptable level. Do you have someone in your team who is dragging everyone down? Or someone who is swallowing up your time because their work needs to be constantly checked before it goes out? Or a person who refuses to make decisions or use their initiative?

Managing poor performers is a difficult, time-consuming job. To obtain the best outcome get on to it early and approach the problem in a systematic way. In this section we will take a step-by-step approach.

Step 1: Analyse the poor performance and its history

First of all, describe the poor performance – be very specific and note down examples. Now, check that the performance really is below an acceptable level and that the person is not simply at the tail end of a very good team. Dealing with genuine poor performance is different from wanting to encourage a mediocre performer to do better.

Next, note any tasks that the person is performing at an acceptable level. Is the poor performance pervasive or is it, on the other hand, limited to only certain aspects of their role?

Poor performers often start quite well before the decline sets in. So try to recall when the problem began and what was happening around that time. If you have taken on the team leader role very recently, talk to their former manager if that is possible.

Another thing to keep in mind is that the poor performance is not necessarily the fault of the person. For example, there might be a broader workflow issue that is preventing them from doing their job properly, so try to keep an open mind. You will find some other possible causes later in this section. Some are attributable to the poor performer while others point to things that require your leadership to rectify.

Step 2: Meeting with the poor performer

Give the poor performer notice of the meeting, tell them what it is about (they are unlikely to be surprised), and organise a confidential place to meet.

Start by repeating the purpose of the meeting, what you want from it, and the kind of conversation you hope to have. For example:

> 'As you know, two of our customers have raised concerns with how you are managing their accounts. Today I want to discuss your work performance with you and identify some areas where you can improve. I want to hear your views and work with you to resolve these problems...'

A simple introduction like this puts the discussion into a problem-solving and collaborative mode. You want them to open up rather than close down and be defensive.

Next, discuss the issues, one by one if necessary. Your preparation from Step 1 will be your guide. Listen carefully because the person will naturally see some issues differently from you – you want to bring your understandings closer together, not further apart. Your aim is to reach some form of agreement as to the poor performance issues. Be as firm as you have to be.

In the final part of the meeting your aim is to devise a performance improvement plan that targets the issues you have identified together. The more focused and specific this is, the more likely it is to work. Write down the things you have agreed to. The discussion might end like this:

> 'So today we have agreed that you will stay in regular contact with each of your account customers. You will organise your files better so that no one slips through the cracks. You have decided to draw up a spreadsheet listing each contact, to whom you will speak at least once per week and record a summary of your discussions. We will meet up this time next week to review your progress and at agreed intervals after that. I am always available if there is anything you want to discuss between meetings.'

Before jumping to solutions, try to identify the causes of the poor performance. Knowing what is triggering the problem takes you a long way towards solving it. Here are four factors that could be implicated:

Person – job fit

- lack of aptitude for this kind of work
- insufficient job-related knowledge
- outmoded skill set
- lack of experience or know-how.

Motivation

- lack of interest in some aspects of the role
- problems with the way the job is designed
- the person feels unrewarded, unrecognised or undervalued.

Role clarity

- performance expectations are unclear to the person
- person does not understand the priorities
- roles in the team overlap and there is confusion/conflict over responsibilities
- there are workflow problems between this person and others in the team
- roles outside work (e.g. as parent) conflict with work requirements.

Support

- person does not have the resources they need
- expectations of the person are unrealistically high
- the team climate is poor
- leadership is lacking in some way.

As you can see from these lists, sometimes the cause of the poor performance has to do with the skills, knowledge or attitudes of the person. At other times it beyond their control. Think about Frank's situation in the 'fresh and frozen' department. He was unhappy that frozen goods were sometimes stacked higher than the line specified in the containers and, as a result, some of the food was spoiling. Initially, he assumed that the staff were either untrained in the correct standards or simply negligent. As it turned out, it was a systemic problem to do with bottlenecks in the way the work flowed when deliveries arrived at awkward times.

It is easy to fall into the trap of blaming someone and counselling them for poor performance when they are not in full control of the factors affecting their work. This is something to keep in mind at performance appraisal time, too.

Step 3: Follow up

Poor performers generally need closer supervision and more frequent feedback than others. By following up, you are signalling that you are serious about seeing a change for the better and that you take your role as leader and coach very seriously. Acknowledge improvement when you see it but also pick up on continuing problems. Review progress at the agreed time, adjust performance improvement plans, and continue with this process for as long as necessary.

Over to you

Your main role as a leader is to ensure your team stays productive. It is your 'value add'. If things are not getting done, resources are not used efficiently, or if your style is too laissez-faire, then you are not doing your job. You are there to actively ensure that your team's goals and priorities are aligned with your organisation's strategy. The three approaches in this chapter to getting your people and team focused on the things that matter should cover most issues or dilemmas that come up.

The first approach is to ensure role clarity. Each person in the team needs to know what is expected of them and their contribution to the team. Work flows within the team also need to be optimised – one of the main purposes of team building. As leader, you will find that the two processes suggested – **role and responsibility charting** and **the team dynamics checklist** – will cover most of your needs in building your team. The former will help ensure that team members are working efficiently together, while the latter is a check on the social dynamics that affect the quality of the work.

The second approach is to get the best out of the performance management (appraisal) system used in your organisation. By knowing the potential pitfalls of performance appraisal and being organised in the ways suggested, you should find it a valuable process for setting goals and standards, and acknowledging effort and results.

Finally, few leaders are fortunate enough to have a team where everyone's contribution is as it should be. That is why the final approach suggested in this chapter is to manage poor performers by intervening early, gaining agreement about aspects of performance that need to be improved and sticking to your performance improvement plan.

Chapter 6
Energise and motivate the team

*Life can be pulled by goals just as surely
as it can be pushed by drives.*

Viktor Frankl

In this chapter ...

You will find out how to energise and motivate your team by
implementing three complementary reward strategies. This is the
second of the three domains (recommended in this book) where you
should aim to develop your knowledge and capabilities as an effective
leader.

Rewarding your team

Inspiring leaders excel at lifting the capability and performance of their teams
to the highest levels. In doing so, energising and motivating the team is
just as important as focusing individual and team effort on the things that
matter. The two leadership behaviours work in tandem.

You will need a comprehensive motivation and reward strategy to succeed in
this. It will be about appreciating contributions, acknowledging results and
encouraging effort. When you reward people they want to do more of what
is good for the business and steer away from behaviours that are wasteful
or unproductive. In short, rewarding your team is what you do to motivate
them – it helps people perform to their potential. Why does rewarding

people work? Another word for 'reward' is 'reinforcement' and as this word implies, behaviour that is reinforced in more likely to be repeated. Reward people when they do what you want them to do and their focus will shift in that direction.

Sometimes as leader you are directly involved in providing the reward – for example, by setting up an 'employee of the month' scheme. At other times you are more in the background, ensuring that the conditions are right for people to feel the satisfaction of using their favourite skills, meeting a challenge or helping a client with a difficult problem. There is no single approach to motivating people. You need a tool kit with diverse strategies. That is why this chapter explains three different strategies for rewarding and motivating your team and provides guidelines on how to implement each one.

What are the best rewards? The answer is simple – they are things that have value for the person on the receiving end. A reward has value because it satisfies a need. Earlier, we looked at Alderfer's ERG theory, with its existence, relatedness and growth need groupings. We all have needs in each of these groups and we hope and expect that many of them will be satisfied through our work. However, the rewards that have the most potential to bring out the best in people are relatedness and growth needs. People who are energised and motivated experience the social climate at work as highly positive and supportive, they truly enjoy their tasks and they see a genuine purpose in what they do.

Think about the lessons of your own experience by considering a recent situation when you felt rewarded by your manager for something you did. What happened? How did you feel? It feels good when your hard work is recognised, it boosts your self-esteem and re-energises you. So here is your first lesson – what counts the most is the experience of being acknowledged or appreciated. We cannot get enough of it but, sadly, many leaders fail to show sufficient interest or give any indication that they have noticed.

Think back again on the experience. What form did the reward take? Was it a salary rise, a better computer or a simple 'thank you'? It does not matter very much, as long as you valued it. If it had no value for you, or seemed insultingly meagre, then it would not register with you as a reward at all. So here is the second lesson from your experience – to be a reward, it has to be of value to the person receiving it. This does not mean that rewards have to be 'big'. In fact, words of appreciation always work but they may not be sufficient if the achievement merited something of greater value.

Again, reflecting on your own experience, how did you know that the reward you received was due to a particular achievement? This might seem like a silly question. Perhaps in your case the reason for the reward was quite explicit. What often happens, though, is that leaders try to reward team members but they miss the mark because they are too vague in explaining what the reward is for, or the gap in time between the achievement and the reward is too great. There is little impact. Here is a short scenario to illustrate the point:

> *Carl stood waiting for the lift to arrive when his boss chanced by. She had been meaning to set up another meeting with him, apparently, but her schedule was always too crowded. 'But let me take this opportunity to say how pleased I was with your work on Phase 1 of the town centre redevelopment project.' She went on to say that she would recommend Carl for a raise, before disappearing into the lift.*
>
> *Carl hurried to his office feeling rather pleased with himself – he could really use the extra money to buy accessories for his SUV. Fortunately, she seemed to have forgotten about the earlier problem of the slow commercial development approvals, now solved, thanks to some great teamwork. He also thought about the town centre redevelopment project. It was a complex project that had taken several months to get through Phase 1. Was there some aspect of it, such as the community consultation or the on-time completion, that she particularly liked, or was she just happy with the overall result? Anyway, he was keen to get back to the team and pass on the praise, and especially to Alex, who had put in a lot of time and effort.*

Carl has had a good encounter with his boss. She acknowledged his good work and promised a pay rise. On the other hand, she missed an opportunity to reinforce specific aspects of his work and coach him towards even greater achievements. Her other fault is that she did not make the time to talk to

Carl sooner, leaving this discussion to a chance encounter. So here is your third lesson – rewards work best when the recipient sees a clear link between them and specific behaviours or achievements.

To summarise, this is what you already know from past experience:

- ✓ What counts the most is the experience of being acknowledged or appreciated.
- ✓ To be a reward, it has to be of value to the person receiving it.
- ✓ Rewards work best when the recipient sees a clear link between them and specific behaviours or achievements.

Motivating for results

Rewarding and motivating your team takes careful thought and planning. You need to know which behaviours or levels of performance you want to encourage and have a clear, consistent strategy for rewarding them when they occur.

Some leaders take a scattergun approach – they liberally dispense praise, bonhomie, invitations to drinks after work, or anything else at their disposal to buoy up the atmosphere in the hope that some of it will produce the right result. This might create a feel-good atmosphere for a while but it is unlikely to translate into substantial results. A more deliberate or targeted approach works better in most situations.

Reward behaviours that contribute to the outcomes you want

Every team that succeeds does so for different reasons. Success is not necessarily just about working harder or staying at work late. Depending on the nature of the task it might be the determination to find a solution, creativity, genuine concern for the client or a high level of attention to detail.

Let us assume that your new team performs well at least some of the time. Can you list the things that they do well? These are among your team's strengths and are the behaviours that you should continue to reinforce as a key component of your motivation strategy. Strengths sustain high levels of performance over the longer term.

Next, notice the people and behaviours you pay most attention to and those that fall beneath your radar. Are you favouring the most visible members of the team at the expense of the good people who quietly get on with the job? Are some people putting too much effort into things that are unimportant, wasteful or unnecessary? Are you rewarding such behaviours inadvertently, for instance by praising people who come in early, even though they spend the extra time on personal business? If this is happening take a positive approach and redirect efforts towards tasks that need to be done. Then reward them.

Now, try to pinpoint aspects of team performance that you would like to improve. Perhaps the team is enthusiastic in the early stages of a project but efforts taper off in the middle. There might be too much wastage of time or materials. Necessary procedures might not be followed correctly. Deadlines might rarely be met. Or staff might like making the sale but avoid the paperwork or restocking. The possibilities are numerous. If you are clear about what these problems are, you are better able to make decisions about plugging the gap and encouraging behaviours that will bring in a better result.

In brief, do these things to focus your team's behaviours on the outcomes you want:

- ✓ Know your team's strengths and build on them.
- ✓ Recognise and reward behaviours that contribute to outcomes and redirect activities that do not.
- ✓ Identify areas where you want performance to improve and use positive strategies to build capability.
- ✓ Reward collaborative team effort.

What distinguishes great teams from ordinary ones? They are energised and productive and consistently outperform their peers and the competition. They take pride in the quality of their work and are eager to learn. In teams where success depends on people cooperating closely, they are more than willing to share their skills and knowledge. They don't like to waste resources and they care about their clients or customers. Ordinary teams are very different. They do what they have to do, put less value on sharing and learning and often have to do the job again because it wasn't good enough the first time around.

None of the things that make teams great happen by accident. Of course, it helps to have a good mix of skills and it does take time for people to work smoothly together. Then again, some teams never make it, despite the individual talents of their members or the months or years they spend together. And, as discussed previously, the team's focus and social dynamics need to be sound. However, to get optimal performance and results, additional reward and motivation strategies are essential. Think of motivation as the fine oil that allows the machinery to operate at peak performance – and what happens if the oil runs out.

Take a look at your team and notice if they are energised and productive. Do they support one another's efforts and share resources or is there an undercurrent of competition dragging the team down? Do they care about clients and customers or is near enough, good enough? And most important of all, is your leadership the difference between an ordinary team and a great one? So, as part of your motivation strategy, be sure to reinforce their collaborative efforts.

Here are some ways to reward collaborative team effort:

- ✓ Encourage each person to feel significant and part of a community.
- ✓ Instil a culture of shared learning and accomplishment.
- ✓ Focus on strategies to meet each person's relatedness needs.

Reward persistence when things get tough

Motivated teams do all of the work, not just the interesting, fun things. Great teams keep at it until the job is done. Someone is always prepared to do the boring, less glamorous stuff that is only noticed if it is neglected. They don't give up easily and persist until they find a way around any obstacles that get in the way. For them, a problem is a challenge, not a reason to throw in the towel. When things don't turn out as well as they had hoped, they are determined to do it better next time.

When highly motivated, teams are also willing to go the extra mile for their customers by meeting difficult timelines, ensuring that things are done properly and following through. They'll even elect to stay back to fix things, without you having to steel yourself and ask someone. In short, highly motivated people sometimes feel the strain and experience frustration but their desire to solve the problem or make things better sees them through. They are happy to accept a bit of pain along the way.

It is easy to be a leader when the waters are smooth. The military leader Sir William Slim said that the real test of leadership is not if your people will follow you in success, but if they will stick by you in defeat and hardship. It is about what happens when you hit a rough patch. How did you perform as a leader last time the pressure was on due to an unexpected turn of events, like funding cuts or the emergence of a stiff competitor? Were you able to keep the team on deck or did it turn into a race for the lifeboats?

Try these ideas to reward persistence when things get tough:

- ✓ Organise a team celebration after meeting a difficult goal or overcoming an obstacle.
- ✓ Pay attention to people who do the necessary work that others avoid.
- ✓ Remind the team often about the higher, shared purpose that makes their efforts worthwhile.

The three strategies for rewarding and motivating

Jobs that provide for the satisfaction of relatedness and growth needs (higher level needs) are usually more rewarding and motivating than those that provide only for existence needs (lower level needs). However, existence needs are important too, because a feeling of safety and security around the conditions at work feeds into to a positive social climate. The satisfaction of existence needs is therefore an important building block for employee engagement. The challenge for leaders is to create and maintain a situation where team members are able to satisfy needs from all three groups.

Getting the settings right is not easy for leaders to do, and for the most obvious of reasons – it is work we are talking about and not free time. People are employed to do tasks that others want them to do. They enter a work agreement and their behaviour falls under the authority of other people. Consider the difference between doing something at home, for a hobby, say, and doing the same thing for a job. This might be cooking, repairing furniture or gardening. At home we do things for ourselves and the people we love and are essentially our own boss. We have the freedom to choose what to do, when and how. At work, on the other hand, a lot gets in the way – the boss, the work environment, the rules. Think of the terms that are used to describe people who work for others – workhorse, wage slave, serf – with their images of drudgery, feeling captive and exhaustion. These terms do not describe jobs as well as they might have 100 years ago but the point remains – doing something for a hobby is more fun than doing it for a salary.

That is why every leader needs a carefully planned approach to rewarding and motivating their staff and for making the work experience as natural and enjoyable as possible.

So, the three planks of your reward strategy are:

- Use workplace rewards and inducements.
- Design jobs that satisfy higher level needs.
- Link work to core values.

Strategy 1: Use workplace rewards and inducements

Simply having a job is very attractive to most people. A job provides a reason to get up in the morning, a source of income, friendships, opportunities to accomplish something worthwhile and a sense of purpose, among other things.

Modern management operates within this reality by providing inducements (things that satisfy the needs of workers) in return for contributions (efforts that workers put in). Every employer offers an array of inducements including salary, other monetary rewards, work-life balance provisions, leave entitlements, training, opportunities for advancement, and more. These are often referred to as **extrinsic rewards** – benefits that come with a particular type of job, but which are largely separate from the actual work content.

As a leader you have considerable discretion over how to apply the extrinsic rewards that your company has on offer. It comes with the power of your position. You can, for example, recommend a salary increment when the person has worked well. You can send people to training courses or help them further their career. You can do this generously and be viewed by your team as a supportive and encouraging leader. Or you can go about it in a mean spirited way, for example by disallowing leave for no obvious reason or frowning on requests to use an entitlement to a work-life balance activity.

You also have a wide range of simple and subtle measures at your disposal to reward and motivate your team. Everything you do to guide and acknowledge effort counts. It can be as simple as a few words of advice, talking to a person about the task they are doing, passing on compliments from senior management and giving feedback on what customers are saying.

In practice: Using workplace rewards and inducements

With the extrinsic rewards you have a wide range of company policies and your skill as a leader to draw on. Notice your own patterns when it comes to rewarding your staff and be mindful of the strategies you use the most, or the least. Be careful to target your reward strategies at the behaviours you really want and use disincentives, like docking pay, only as a last resort.

Here are some more pointers for your workplace motivation strategy.

Be seen to be fair
If you do nothing else as a leader, be even-handed and transparent. Nothing is more demotivating for people than the perception that rewards are

distributed unfairly, that the boss is playing favourites or that someone's contributions are not recognised along with other people's.

It's not just about the money
Leaders often equate rewards with pay rises and monetary incentives and give up trying to reward people because they don't have enough control over the finances. They fail to realise that productive workplaces are often characterised by the generous use of more subtle encouragements. Rewards come in many shapes and sizes. Don't underestimate the value of rewards like praise, a simple thankyou or the chance to work on an interesting project. Recognition and challenge can be very powerful motivators for the right people.

Make 'rewards' valuable to the recipient
It is only a reward if it has value for the person on the receiving end. You might want to attend a conference in Tahiti but, although it is hard to imagine, not everyone would! A reward is anything that satisfies a need. Our needs come in many shapes and sizes. Money is a great reward because we use it to satisfy many basic needs like food and housing, and a high salary conveys success and status. But our relatedness needs are also very important, so group outings or being invited to contribute to a group project can be powerful motivators. Rewards that satisfy higher needs like self-esteem include 'employee of the month', acknowledgement for playing a key role and being asked to mentor a junior colleague.

So, the reward has to be something worth having and it has to be big enough to spur potential recipients to action. In some organisations, for instance, good people don't apply for promotions because the small amount of additional salary is not worth the extra hours and responsibility, as they see it. So don't insult people by offering peanuts when they feel they have earned a full meal!

Make the right connections between effort and reward
There must be a clear connection between the effort or result, and the reward that comes from it. Don't just assume that people know that the bonus, special project or bigger office was the result of something that they did. Be explicit – let them know why, exactly.

Monkeys demand equal pay[25]

Experiments with animals sometimes provide interesting insights into human behaviour. Sarah Brosnan from Georgia State University has conducted laboratory experiments to see how capuchin monkeys, a highly social primate species, respond when they are treated unfairly.

Picture this scene during one of the experiments. Two monkeys sit in adjacent enclosures with a clear view of each other and the human experimenter outside. The monkeys know the task – on receipt of a token from the experimenter they go to the corner of their enclosure, pick up a stone and hand it to her. The experimenter then gives them a reward, a slice of cucumber (acceptable reward) or a grape (more desirable reward).

Things start well. The monkey on the left completes the task, is given cucumber and eats it (tastes okay). She then watches as the monkey on the right does the same task and is given a grape (yum!). It is the turn of the first monkey again. She completes the task and gets more cucumber. This time she refuses to eat it and throws it down. She watches again as the other monkey completes the task and receives another grape. On the third and fourth rounds the first monkey is offered cucumber. She hurls it back at the experimenter, bangs her fist on the floor and rattles her cage.

Like many primates, we humans have a sense of fairness that is deeply ingrained in our psyche. We compare ourselves to others in the same situation and make assessments about how equitably we are treated. We do not like to be short changed, and if we are we respond by acting out our frustration, 'having words' with management, or retreating into our corners.

Animal experiments like these with the capuchin monkeys show that a sense of fairness has an evolutionary basis, a human universal that is not particular to certain cultures or societies.

Inequity or unfairness elicits very strong emotional reactions, including feelings of disgust or repugnance. As a leader, it is important that you are seen to be fair.

The connection can get lost for all sorts of reasons. Rewards are often given inconsistently – sometimes they are given, and sometimes not, or too much time separates achievement and reward. People have only vague recollections of what it was for. It is nice to get, but it doesn't make much difference to their performance.

Don't confuse happiness and motivation

Being rewarded for effort and results is satisfying. As leader, you want your team to feel satisfied because of work performance and results above all else. Other things can be satisfying too, like a view over the harbour, friendly colleagues, free parking and a good salary. These things can make coming to work a lot more pleasant but they don't necessarily have much impact on performance (unless they are explicitly built in as incentives). The worst scenario is for people to be happy and satisfied for all the wrong reasons – cushy job, no responsibility and a boss who doesn't notice.

This point is so important it bears repeating – to be effective as motivators, rewards must follow from effort and/or results. It's no good trying to induce more out of people who are not performing by rewarding them up front. They won't do more out of gratitude to you. They might like you better, but that is about it.

Follow through on promises

Following from the point above, it's okay to make promises but don't deliver until the results are in. If you make explicit or implied promises of rewards to come, follow through. Be very clear with people about the give–receive equation. Companies sometimes do things like create the expectation of a bonus or reward but can't deliver for business reasons when the time comes. This leads to resentment – don't expect your team to understand – this is not an issue that sparks a rational response.

Focus on the positives

A similar caveat applies in the case of punishments or disincentives. Only apply the stick when behaviours are consistently unacceptable and are resistant to other methods. Overuse of punishment creates fear and resentment that may come back to bite you. W. Edwards Deming[26], who pioneered Total Quality Management, insisted that managers should 'drive out fear' if they wanted the best out of people. Even Sun Tzu, thousands of years ago, stressed positive means of motivating the troops – no mention of shooting the stragglers. Someone will always be running last. Reduce the gap between them and the pack by using individual performance management (see Chapter 5 for ideas on how to manage poor performers).

Balance team and individual incentives
Getting the right balance between individual and team rewards is crucial but difficult to do. You won't win the game if half the team is turned off or doesn't care. Too much emphasis on team incentives may leave the most productive people feeling aggrieved, while encouraging complacency at the tail end. On the other hand, an almost exclusive use of individual rewards will undermine team effort. To be productive, a team needs to pool the available talent in an environment where people help each other to be their best.

Strategy 2: Design jobs that satisfy higher level needs

Think about the most appealing aspects of your job or the best moments that you can remember. Consider only those things that are about the work itself, rather than the particular company where you were employed. Your list is likely to include important achievements, using or developing your favourite skills, or being able to deliver real benefits to your customers or clients. Sure, a fat salary with a high-status company are things that might have attracted you in the first place but what sustains and motivates you over the longer term is the quality of the work itself.

These are **intrinsic job rewards**. They are tied to the content of the job, including your level of interest in the work, the degree of challenge, decision-making responsibility and opportunities for professional growth. Notice that these factors are aligned with Alderfer's growth needs. A 'good' job is loaded up with opportunities to experience intrinsic rewards. Jobs like this have far more **motivational potential** than jobs that provide for the satisfaction of lower level needs only.

Deliberately designing jobs to be intrinsically rewarding is a relatively new phenomenon and is one of the best things you can do to encourage high-quality work. People who are genuinely engaged in what they are doing do not need to be managed closely. However, they do like to feel in control of their work day – they like to share decision-making responsibility and work well with leaders who use a coaching or mentoring style.

Do not make the mistake of thinking that your people are less interested in intrinsic satisfaction than you, yourself, are. Surveys show that people at all levels and in all occupations like to have jobs that are interesting and challenging. Here are some ideas for building intrinsic quality into the jobs of the people in your team.

In practice: Designing high-quality jobs

As the leader, you do not have direct or immediate control over another person's intrinsic satisfaction, but you can design jobs that contain such potential. The **Job Characteristics Model**[27] is a good tool for doing this and it can be adapted to most occupations and workplaces. You can use it as a yardstick for gauging the motivational potential of the jobs in your team, and as a reminder of the intrinsic rewards that you should be building into the roles of team members.

From the 1960s onwards, many people including Fred Emery[28] and his colleagues worked with organisations redesigning jobs so that they would be more intrinsically satisfying. At that time Theory X attitudes predominated and most jobs were simple, dull and repetitive. They used the Job Characteristics Model to collect information about job quality, assess what was lacking – for example, decision-making responsibility – and design measures to rectify the problem.

According to Emery's version of the model, well-designed jobs provide:

- ✓ variety and challenge
- ✓ elbow room for decision making
- ✓ feedback on performance and results
- ✓ mutual support and respect

✓ wholeness and meaning

✓ room to grow and develop.

Notice that most of the items in this list correspond to Alderfer's growth needs. You can use the above list to assess any kind of job and at any level. The model also has a well-developed methodology[29] for measuring the level of each characteristic but you do not need this to get a good sense of how people in your team feel about their work. What you do need is a basic understanding of each characteristic and a willingness to consult openly with team members about improvements that would make a difference. Talk to people, listen, assess, ask for their ideas.

According to Emery any job can be a 'good' job – it does not have to be a high-status position or one that requires professional training or expertise. Within every job there is scope to motivate people to do their best and to reward that effort. Even if the work itself is not particularly interesting or pleasant, the job holder can be trusted to make appropriate decisions, to be a valued member of the team and to know that what they do is necessary and worthwhile. Often, that is enough.

The table on the next page gives some suggestions for factoring each characteristic into a job.

The information in the table is just a start and you could add more ideas for your situation. Consider such things as the level of expertise and experience of team members – a relatively inexperienced person will need closer supervision and more frequent feedback than one who is confident enough to check in with you less regularly. Also, avoid making assumptions about their understanding of the priorities, how much discretion they feel they have to make decisions, what they know about the needs of customers, and so on. Play it safe and over-communicate on these issues. Keep your lists handy, add to them, and run them past your team from time to time to ensure that the motivational potential of their roles is all it could be.

Job Characteristics Model

Job characteristic	How to factor it in
Variety & challenge	Ensure that the range of tasks or skills needed is wide enough to maintain interest & is of sufficient complexity.
	Include tasks that the person really enjoys doing.
	Provide goals & targets that stretch the job holder, but not so much as to discourage them.
Elbow room	Within reason, allow the person to make decisions about how to do their own work.
	Trust the person to get on with the job without looking over their shoulder.
	Allow teams to share decision making with you & delegate as much as possible.
Feedback on performance	Clarify job roles & provide your feedback frequently.
	Ensure that people know what customers or clients think of the product or service.
	Give both positive & negative feedback.
	Explain reasons for your feedback & decisions.
	Discuss priorities & explain changes of plan.
Mutual support & respect	Ensure that roles in the team are complementary & that work flows smoothly.
	Foster a collaborative & supportive social climate.
	Celebrate successes as a team.
	Elicit & listen to the ideas put forward by the team.
	Value all team roles, not just those in the forefront.

Wholeness & meaning	Ensure that every team member understands their contribution to the overall effort & is valued for it.
	Ensure all understand the value of the product or service to the customer.
	Link individual effort with overall team or organisational values.
Room to grow & develop	Encourage people to see their jobs as steps towards a desirable future.
	Provide each person with opportunities to build on their strengths.
	Link individual needs with development opportunities.

You might wonder about the motivational potential of the jobs in the teams that Margo, Carl and Frank lead. Margo's physiotherapists have plenty of variety, challenge and elbow room. Because of their close connection with their patients and other health professionals they also receive immediate feedback about how much they are helping. Where Margo could do more is in relation to the other three job characteristics. She has made a good start and needs to continue in her efforts towards team member participation in planning and developing the service, linking the team's contributions with professional and organisational values, and assisting people to develop and grow.

Carl, too, is making progress. He is starting to realise that most people need a challenge and enough variety in their work day to maintain their interest. He now understands that receiving feedback is very motivating and that everyone, not just the few, responds well to opportunities for professional development. If he can reduce perceptions that he favours some people (Jon) over others (Alex) the team will develop a greater capacity for mutual support and respect. Carl still needs to work on the last of the job characteristics, wholeness and meaning.

Frank started out with a leadership style that was fairly controlling. That limited the level of motivational potential of the jobs of team members at the supermarket. If you look at the list of job characteristics, you will see that their jobs would not have rated well on any of them. Now that Frank is loosening the controls and doing more to empower the team, the quality of their jobs, in terms of motivational potential, will almost certainly rise.

Strategy 3: Link work to core values

Having a strong sense of purpose, especially one that is shared with others, increases employee engagement. So your third motivational strategy is to tap into your team's core values – the things that you and they really care about. People who can link their work activities with things that matter to them are generally enthusiastic and inspired, far more so than if they are simply working for the money or on someone else's dream.

To link work with core values, you need two elements in your strategy:

Fostering personal and team values: People are more engaged when they share a common understanding of what unites them and a commitment to making things happen for the good of the team as a whole. Fostering team values is about bringing the mission and purpose of your team to life and supporting that with measures that maintain a positive social climate.

Encouraging professional identity and values: Everyone has a core professional identity that is moulded by education, experience, self-concept and personal values. Professionals internalise certain obligations and standards that are independent of company policies and expectations. So create a culture where people are inspired to be their best as fully rounded professionals with something worthwhile to contribute.

This old story about two bricklayers on the same building site will help to distinguish these two kinds of values. In the story each bricklayer was asked what he was doing. The first bricklayer said that he was building a wall, while the second replied that he was a religious man building a cathedral. What is the significance of their different answers, and does it matter if both are equally skilful tradesmen?

The easy assumption to make is that the second bricklayer is motivated by higher values and therefore is more likely than the other to work diligently and with purpose towards the ultimate goal of completing the cathedral.

But let us assume that the first bricklayer cares little for cathedrals and is not inspired by the prospect of seeing one emerge from the chaos of the building site. Does that mean he is less engaged or productive than the other bricklayer? Not necessarily. He might be preoccupied with the quality of the mortar, precision in placing the bricks and other factors that make bricklaying more skilled than the casual observer might assume. Getting the process right is important to him as a professional – quality along the way counts for more than the final outcome.

One bricklayer is motivated by personal and team values, while mastery and professional pride in an exacting process is more significant to the other. Both are important. That is why your motivation and reward strategy should reflect both.

In practice: Linking work with professional and team values

Would you prefer to work in a team where success means something and is celebrated, or in one where people have nothing more than a tick-a-box attitude towards completing each task, crossing it off a long list before moving on to the next? Assuming that it is the former, you will want to unite the team by linking the ultimate purpose of their work with values that are important to them.

Think about your own team – can you identify the purpose in the work that gives it real meaning and value to them? The difference they make to the lives of customers and clients? The times when they were energised or inspired by their results, contributions or progress along the way? You will find the answers to these questions from your observations and, in particular, the conversations you have with people from inside and outside the team. Take your time and do a lot of listening. In the end you will have the makings of a set of messages that you will want to reinforce.

Your messages will need to relate in some way to the larger purpose of your organisation or department. However, do not rely solely on official company communications for your team's vision. Corporate values and mission statements often leave employees cold if they are thought up by senior executives removed from the action. For example, statements about increasing sales by this or that per cent or becoming the world's most respected manufacturer of widgets are not relevant or interesting to most employees. They are just too sterile or abstract. People need something that they can relate to in the here and now.

Your aim is to have a vision with real meaning so that your team has some common ideas, standards or values that focus their minds on a higher purpose, over and above the everyday. You could include one or more of the following components:

- ✓ 'how we do things together' (team culture)
- ✓ 'what we strive to achieve' (goals or outcomes)
- ✓ 'how high we aim' (standards)
- ✓ 'a great place to work' (social climate)
- ✓ 'who we serve' (special client or customer groups)
- ✓ 'why we care' (what makes it worthwhile).

How would Margo, Carl and Frank help their teams to find purpose and value in their work? It should be easy for Margo – her team works with other health professionals to improve the quality of life of very ill children. The physiotherapists are aware of this but Margo needs to bring the importance of their work into the foreground so they share their successes as a team and are inspired by them.

Carl also has plenty of scope to create a vision for his team. It is responsible for assessing proposals from business proprietors and developers relating to new or existing commercial developments in his local government area. Developments that are well conceived and designed can help a town or city centre to become a thriving community. Right now some members of his team are working on a major project – a town centre redevelopment. In the past, the team has tended to take more of a routinised, tick-a-box approach to completing each assessment. Carl has an opportunity to lift their sights by reframing their work as central to creating a vibrant and successful community. There are also many things he can do to improve the social climate and increase perceptions that his department is a great place to work.

Frank's team is involved in a daily cycle of unloading deliveries, storing goods, restocking supermarket shelves, and so on. You might wonder where vision comes in, if at all. If you look at the list above, starting with 'how we do things together', you might imagine some of the messages that could resonate with the team. Frank has started to encourage people to work with him to streamline work processes (team culture), he is attempting to coach the team towards better food handling procedures (standards) and he wants everyone to do their best for the people they serve (customer groups). Over time he should find that attitudes within the team change, and that some common understandings of what they are achieving together gain traction.

Is it necessary to have a mission or purpose if extrinsic and intrinsic reward strategies are already in place? The short answer is 'yes'. Those other strategies are always appropriate, but sometimes more is needed to lift your team's performance. Consider situations where the team is challenged by unexpected delays, seemingly insurmountable obstacles, and changes of plan. At these times the usual carrots have less power – the team just needs to keep persisting. This is where strong team culture comes into play and seeing the job through to completion is a matter of pride and an expression of belief in what the individual and team stands for. It simply makes more sense to put yourself out for your colleagues or clients if you feel a part of a team that has a real purpose.

The other component of your motivation strategy is to encourage professional identity and values. Many professionals, such as accountants, journalists and teachers, internalise certain protocols and standards as a consequence of their professional training. Frequently, they identify as closely with their profession as they do with the company that employs them. With some experience behind them, they can generally be relied upon to get on with the job without much direction. In short, professionals are usually self-managing and set high standards for themselves.

This is of great benefit to organisations that rely on their services. Other things being equal, professionals often put in additional time and effort to complete a job, even when some of the extrinsic rewards that others might insist on are lacking. In some situations they will put themselves to considerable inconvenience or even take personal risks for the sake of the job and especially for the people they serve. There are many examples. Think of people who work in the emergency services, hospitals and some social service organisations.

In everyday situations professionals often keep working because they have the expertise to do the job properly; a client would miss out if they did not continue, or they didn't believe this is something that is worth doing. Why do they do it? Often it is simply because 'that's the kind of thing a person like me does', and not because there is a bonus, pat on the back or any kind of extrinsic or intrinsic reward at the end. It might even look like altruism. In the end it comes back to professional identity and what that means to the individual.

You might think that good professionals require little active leadership from you. On the contrary, they need as much as anyone else. They respond in the same way to a positive social climate and appreciate your feedback and a word of thanks just like other people. Actually, professionals are often at risk of stress and burnout, sometimes because they work too long or hard, but also because they lack sufficient managerial or social support to help them through. In fact, conscientious and dedicated professionals are generally at higher risk than their more easy-going colleagues.

So do what you can to value the contributions of these valuable team members. Here are some suggestions:

- ✓ Create a supportive team culture when everyone feels included.
- ✓ Value people, publicly and privately, for their skills and professional standards.

- ✓ Show concern for each person's needs, professional development and career aspirations.
- ✓ As much as possible, give each person control over their own work.
- ✓ Be active in relation to situations where administrative requirements conflict with professional standards, e.g. when quality time with clients is compromised by cutbacks.
- ✓ Ensure that the physical work environment is congenial, e.g. airy and properly furnished.
- ✓ Be alert to the signs of stress and burnout.

 ## Over to you

We started this chapter with the rather obvious observation that people are motivated when they are rewarded for their efforts. After all, people like other living creatures are attracted to activities that they find satisfying and steer away from situations that they find unpleasant. The problem for you as leader is that when at work, many things get between what people are asked to do during the work day and the feelings of satisfaction that come from it. To really motivate the team, you need a carefully planned strategy to make the vital links between productive effort and the satisfaction of their important needs. People who are motivated are energised, engaged and follow through to get the job done.

This chapter outlined three motivation and reward strategies. As leader you need to include all three as part of your leadership approach. The first strategy is about making best use of the rewards and inducements that your company has available, as well as developing a style of leadership that is supportive and encouraging. The second strategy involves designing jobs that people enjoy doing because they satisfy higher level needs, such as the need to express their creative side or to hone the skills they like to use. The key to engaging your team is to give them as much control over their work as is practicable, provide the right amount of support and show your appreciation.

What will happen if you do not use these two strategies effectively? In general, if you fail to provide intrinsic rewards (tasks that people enjoy doing), team members will not bother putting in as much effort – they will be demotivated. Fail to provide sufficient extrinsic rewards (for example, decent pay and conditions) and they won't feel like coming in to work. This will show up in absenteeism and turnover. If for some reason they can't avoid being there, they will find covert ways of resisting your leadership.

The third strategy is about instilling purpose by linking the work with values that are important to people as professionals or members of a cohesive team. People often do extraordinary things because of a belief that their contributions really count or because of commitments stemming from their professional identity. As the leader, it is up to you to create the conditions for a mutually supportive team culture and an environment where people who find real meaning in their work can thrive.

Chapter 7
Create a positive social climate

We don't fall in line with people who don't respect us and who we don't believe have our best interests at heart. We are willing to follow leaders, but only to the extent that we believe they call on our best, not our worst.

Rachel Maddow

In this chapter ...

You will discover that creating a positive social climate is critical to your success as a leader. Because it impacts trust, openness and engagement, creating a positive social climate is the essential foundation for everything else you do to be effective in your role. This is the third of the three knowledge and capabilities domains (recommended in this book) that you should develop.

One cannot hire a hand

A century ago leaders in organisations were generally distant, aloof and formal. That style fitted the hierarchical nature of roles and work relationships. It's what people expected. Then things began to change in the second part of last century as we discovered more about social dynamics and their impact. People like Mary Parker Follett, Kurt Lewin, Douglas McGregor and Fred Emery opened minds to the idea that collaborative relationships were as important a driver of productivity as technology. These days, it's just common sense but as you know from previous chapters, it took some decades for this idea to take hold.

So what are the present day expectations of leaders when it comes to managing people and teams? If McGregor and the others were here now, they would all agree that people should be treated as fully rounded adults, with their array of attitudes, interests and concerns. Respect would be the cornerstone of any interaction, underpinned by consistency and fair play. Listening carefully, negotiating, coaching and communicating would be crucial.

This is a good place for a reminder of Peter Drucker's[30] observation that one always hires the whole person – a fully rounded adult. People have many time-consuming roles and having a job is just one of them. Depending on your own circumstances you could add parent, MBA student, cricket or netball player, carer, volunteer counsellor, and more. Take a moment to list your main roles and then try to prioritise them. Which one comes out on top? Is it your job or something else?

Until quite recently most people believed the job should take precedence over every other role. If there was a conflict they would juggle their various commitments while giving priority to work. For example, if you had a sick child or elderly parent to care for, you were expected to arrange it without causing inconvenience to your manager or colleagues. Whatever you did it was never enough and you were left feeling guilty. As you can imagine, this was particularly hard on women and sole parents.

Attitudes are changing very quickly. People now view their job as just one role among many. They still value it but work is less likely to be their first priority. They find it unreasonable for management to expect them to make a hard choice between important commitments. They want more latitude to make their own decisions about what to do and when. Some say that Gen Y is leading this trend. Perhaps it is also to do with the changing mix of people in the workforce, broader social change, and the impact of technology on the way we perform work.

We have come a long way on this issue. In McGregor's day individual workers had no scope to change their work hours or to have time away except for those few matters explicitly mentioned under their contracts or awards. If the start time was 8am, work was where they had to be, every day without fail. They were expected to leave their other concerns at the door and absorb themselves fully in the work. Part-time and contract work was relatively rare. The situation was very regimented and it was the same for everyone.

A few decades ago some organisations started to loosen up and allow a degree of flexibility. People could vary their start and finish times, take longer breaks in the middle of the day if necessary and take time out for study, religious observances and family matters. Part-time jobs became common. As more women kept their jobs after marrying, maternity leave was gradually introduced. Now, of course, paternity leave is on the agenda.

As accommodating as these allowances might seem, there were still limits on personal choice because most people were covered by the same set of rule-bound provisions. For example, a policy of the whole team having to be in the office during core hours might not suit a person wanting to attend an afternoon lecture under their study leave entitlement.

This brings us to the present and what we might expect in coming years. Attitudes continue to evolve and the standardised 'one size fits all' approach of years gone by no longer seems adequate. People now expect work conditions and patterns that suit their interests, lifestyles and personal preferences. They want compressed work weeks, days working at home, time off to participate in cultural events, and more. They respond well to work-life balance initiatives as well as workplace arrangements for healthy lifestyles such as gym rooms and health clubs.

This trend towards **individual customisation of work conditions** challenges leaders to shift their thinking towards the results achieved by each team member – their 'value add' – and away from viewing them simply as a job or role occupant. When the leader focuses on contributions and results, it makes sense to consider how to support each person so that they can get on with the job and deliver. As long as the person is reliable, they retain their autonomy and the number of hours spent in the office under direct supervision seems less important, or even arbitrary.

So what does this mean for your leadership?

- ✓ Divide your time across the whole team and not just the people you like or whose company you prefer.
- ✓ When you see an opportunity that would benefit a team member, make sure you connect them with it.
- ✓ Value diversity by bringing more voices into the discussion.
- ✓ Lead from the front and model the behaviours you expect. For example, take your own study leave entitlements, stay at home if you have a nasty virus, and use the company's fitness equipment to help you stay healthy.
- ✓ Be responsive to people's needs to attend cultural events and important milestones in their lives.
- ✓ Be responsive to the needs of those with responsibility for children, disabled relatives and the elderly.

To be hard-nosed about this, there are bottom-line benefits for organisations that actively promote individual customisation of work conditions. The workplace feels more warm and supportive, contributing to a better social climate. There is less 'need' for absenteeism (including unexpected sickies to cover things like attending school concerts, taking elderly parents to the doctor, and so on), and less presenteeism (turning up to work even though the person has an illness). People appreciate a considerate employer and show it through their loyalty and commitment. They are less likely to look around for a better place to work and are more likely to speak well of the organisation when with friends and colleagues. Organisations that have a good image can, and do, use this to attract quality employees.

Emotionally intelligent leadership

Leaders who foster a social climate of trust and support need a good measure of emotional intelligence to engage the team. You have heard this term, but what does it look like in action?

Consider this scenario:

> Garry sat uncomfortably in his chair, planting his phone squarely on the table in front of him and turning it onto silent. He flicked through the papers and stared at the agenda for the fourth time that morning. The item hadn't moved – still item 5 on the new business list. Why did they always put the most important stuff near the bottom? He slowly looked around the table and settled his gaze on Carl, who quickly looked away. No support there then. Phil finally got the meeting off to a start – bloody late as usual – while Garry leaned back in his chair and seconded the minutes he hadn't read.
>
> Item 5, at last! Garry shifted forward in his seat while his grip tightened on his pencil. What could he expect other than a whitewash from the chair and a stupid question from that new bloke Carl? But hang on ... here's Phil asking him to lead off by giving the meeting his take on the issue ... he's been down to the stores recently and chatted with a few of the blokes ... and can see there is a problem meriting serious attention. Well, well, well! Garry rose a little taller in his chair, tapped his pencil on the table and began to lay it on the line.

This is a story told from Garry's perspective, but the one to watch is Phil. Phil is deputy CEO and Garry is one of the managers in his division. He finds Garry a bit abrasive and not much interested in anything except his own team in stores. On the other hand, Garry does his job well and has improved as a leader since his supervision training.

Phil read the situation well. He could see that Garry was pumped up and ready for a fight – his body language gave it away. But how should he handle it? It would have been tempting to meet like with like and use his role as chair to put Garry in his place. He showed great self-control in not doing so. Instead, he was empathic and expressed understanding of the problem in the stores. In response, Garry calmed down. He then invited Garry to explain the situation, a position that Garry did not expect to find himself in. He felt included, and listened to!

This is what emotionally intelligent behaviour is all about – reading the emotional undertones and moulding the interaction to create a favourable environment for solving problems. Phil has demonstrated the necessary skills for us. He picks up on others' emotions. He can make connections between these emotions and the factors that set them off. He chooses the right actions to reduce the heat and influences others to participate in a positive way. And of course he is very self-aware and shows great restraint and self-control. He has all of the capabilities that go with emotionally intelligent leadership, as depicted in the diagram.

Self-awareness
Knowing our own emotions & what causes them

Empathy
Understanding how others feel & anticipating their reactions

Self-control
Managing our emotional responses

Emotionally intelligent leadership

Influence
Changing or improving the emotional climate

Resilience
Bouncing back & managing difficult situations

What would the scenario look like if Phil had handled it differently? Garry would have returned to the stores with steam coming out of his ears and others at the meeting would have felt very uncomfortable. The quality of joint problem solving at future meetings would have been the poorer for it.

The idea that interpersonal skills are as critical to leadership success as thinking ability is fairly new. Daniel Goleman[31] popularised the idea in his 1995 book, *Emotional Intelligence*. It was an idea whose time had come because the emerging style of leadership was all about building partnerships, teamwork and employee engagement. Managers could no longer shelter behind a raft of rigid procedures, technical controls and strict lines of authority. They had to adjust to a world where their people skills were as developed as their capacity to organise and think strategically.

Emotional intelligence (EI) contributes to good leadership in a number of ways. Leaders with higher levels of EI usually have better verbal and non-verbal communication skills. They are good at explaining things, but are particularly adept at doing so when the situation is a bit strained. For example, when they notice a degree of confusion or discomfort in the room – the downward glances, the sideways looks, the reluctance to speak up.

They also respond better in such situations because they are aware of their own feelings and can keep them in check, even when emotions are running a little high. It's easy to get defensive when there is an air of challenge or hostility in the room. But being defensive is a sure way to close down communication. Leaders who stay calm are better able to support their teams and keep moving forward despite some difficult moments.

You behave in an emotionally intelligent way by doing the following:

- ✓ Reflect on your own behaviour after any event involving other people and observe how you felt and interacted.
- ✓ Ask for feedback and advice from people you value.
- ✓ Get to know your strengths and weaknesses as a communicator.
- ✓ Recognise situations where you overreact, and learn to step back and consider your feelings and possible responses before taking action.

✓ Notice how other people feel, observing both their non-verbal and verbal behaviour.

✓ Let people know that you understand how they feel.

✓ Build your resilience as a counter to the stresses of your job.

Leadership in times of stress

Workplace stress can reduce your capacity to operate at your best and to engage with people on a personal level. Numerous surveys have shown that moderate to high levels of work stress are common, especially for people early in their professional career.

Everyone has experienced stress at some time in their lives and a bit of stress before a big event like a sports competition or having to give an important presentation can enhance performance. But when stress is an everyday presence, it wears people down and affects their performance. Over the longer term it is very bad for overall health and wellbeing.

How much stress do you experience in your role? Would you describe it as low, medium or high stress? Do you think it is affecting the way you do your job? Here are some signs that might indicate you are under more stress than you can comfortably handle:

- You are more withdrawn than usual, and the team is noticing that the distance between you and them has increased.
- You are feeling more irritable and impatient than usual.
- Although you seem to be busier than ever, you are accomplishing less.
- You are not concentrating as well as you used to.
- You are failing to consider all angles before making key decisions.
- Your ability to focus on strategy or longer term outcomes is less sharp.
- You feel tired or exhausted a lot of the time.
- You are starting to doubt your ability or effectiveness.

Do any of these apply to you? If so, it could indicate that a moderate to high level of stress is interfering with your effectiveness as a leader. As you can see from the list, too much stress affects relationships, your ability to think clearly, and your energy levels, all for the worse. If you are stressed then your team is noticing it because you are unlikely to be communicating as confidently, openly and supportively as usual. If you have any weak spots, like a tendency to lose your cool, it is more likely to come out when stressed.

For all of these reasons it is important to manage your stress and develop ways to keep it at bay. Some people think that stress is a part of modern work and life and that you simply have to put up with it. Not necessarily so. There is almost always something you can do to feel more in control. So if things are getting you down at work, talk it through with a friend, mentor or coach. They will help you identify situations that trigger your stress and come up with some self-management strategies to help you deal with them.

The other approach to mitigating stress is to build your resilience by making changes to your lifestyle. Resilience is your personal shield against the blows, setbacks and disappointments of life. As a leader, you need it because of the frequent demands and challenges that you face, to stay calm and focused, and to bounce back when things do not turn out as you expect. While there is not the room in this book to cover this area, it is worth investigating the many things that you can do to build your resilience.

Resilience is not just for individuals. Team members often face common pressures and as a group can display similar signs of wear and tear. Individually, and as a team, they need resilience, too. If you think that the team or some individuals are not dealing with things as well as they could, or results are slipping, then too much stress and strain could be a factor. If you think that this is an issue and you do not have the capacity or knowledge to manage it yourself, then seek outside assistance.

Managing difficult relationships

Every leader at one time or another has a difficult person in their team, people like Garry. They can be a real challenge – the kind that you wish would just go away. The reality is that your team is made up of people with a range of personalities, styles and temperaments. Your best option is to use emotionally intelligent behaviour and try to establish constructive relationships with everyone.

A person might be more 'difficult' than most people for a number of reasons. Someone managed poorly in the past might now be rather wary or evasive in their dealings with you. Or another might have had a good relationship with your predecessor with a very different management style from your own. They have not adjusted well and their behaviour implies that they find you wanting as a manager. Then there are the people who are waiting out their time until retirement, and counting the days, much to the chagrin of those around them.

So past circumstances can set patterns that upset relationships in the present. Before taking action you will want to figure out why the person is resisting your leadership. Just being nice to the one who is out of step and trying to win them over may make things worse. Think about it – if the previous manager made all the decisions (and they liked it), your genial attempts to bring them into the circle may make you look weak and indecisive in their eyes. Don't assume that your leadership style will be appreciated by everyone – some people need help in understanding its logic and how it will work for them. Whatever the underlying cause of the problem, it will take time and patience to turn it around.

Personality can also be a factor in workplace relationships. To some extent our behaviour is influenced by patterns formed early in our lives and, as a result, we respond to people and situations in different ways. For example, people with early childhood experiences of having their basic needs met, including strong attachments and feelings of being in control, are generally confident and positive in outlook. Those who were denied, hurt or made to feel insecure are often somewhat hesitant or suspicious in social situations, less self-confident and apprehensive around change.

There are many influences on personality, of course, and people do change over their lifetimes. However, five fairly stable personality characteristics, known as the 'big 5', are relevant to behaviour in organisations. These are defined in the following table.

Big 5 personality factors

Extroversion – introversion	Orientation to the social world of people, relationships & events, as opposed to the inner world of ideas & reflections
Conscientiousness	Extent to which we are organised, reliable, dependable & details-focused
Agreeableness	Extent to which we are friendly, flexible & helpful, as opposed to being hostile towards rules, less of a team player & uncomfortable in social situations
Emotional stability	Degree to which we are secure, resilient & non-reactive
Openness to experience	Extent to which we are open, curious & adaptable to new circumstances

As leader, you will want to know how individual differences on these personality dimensions can influence behaviour in a team. Let's consider the 'emotional stability' dimension. You might have someone who seems volatile and touchy. If this is a regular pattern in their behaviour, the chances are they have less emotionally stability than others. On the other hand, if this pattern has emerged recently, something else is probably going on.

Let's assume for a moment that the behaviour pattern is normal for this person. You can't turn around something that is fundamental to a person's makeup – what you see might be hard to deal with but it is within the normal range of human behaviour. However, you can help the person to moderate their reactions so that they participate more evenly in the team setting. But they do have to trust you, and it might take some time.

What can you do? Assuming that the person has misunderstood something or simply overreacted, your best approach is to stay calm yourself and not fall into the trap of mimicking their behaviour. After they have quietened down, take them aside and talk about the event that upset them, their response, and the impact of their behaviour on other members of the team.

This will be hard but it is important to stay open-minded rather than blaming and judgemental. Be very consistent and predictable in your dealings with this individual – they don't handle surprises very well. Your role is to help them develop some insights into their own behaviour so they can learn to self-manage.

You might also have a team member who is less of a team player than others (a sign of the less 'agreeable' type). This person argues the point long after others are on board, grumbles when asked to help out a team member, refuses to leave the building for fire drill, or acts as if team celebrations are a waste of time. What can you do with a person like this? Trying to coax them into enjoying team relationships and sharing achievements will have limited success. A better approach would be to explain the consequences of their behaviour on team morale and outcomes and be very clear about your expectations of their behaviour. If they really are a drain on the team, consider some of the suggestions for managing poor performers in Chapter 5.

Failing to manage your difficult relationships can turn into a nightmare. It is best to take remedial action early but not before you have developed some insight into the underlying causes of the behaviour. Think about how Phil would manage a team member who tends to fly off the handle when upset, a person who is less cooperative than others, or a team meeting where the atmosphere is a little heated. Wouldn't he remain calm and watchful? Probably. It would be hard though, due to a natural tendency to see the situation as a threat to his leadership, one requiring him to assert his control and authority. However, as an experienced leader, Phil would know it is better not to fall into the trap of pushing back because it would make him appear weak and insecure. He would listen, explain, answer questions and ask for ideas. He would show he is comfortable with differences of opinion and that he does not take it personally. A perfect role model for you.

You might be interested in the other three personality characteristics in the table. Job recruitment agencies who use personality testing often include tests of the 'big 5' because they have been well researched and validated. Conscientiousness is associated with success in a wide range of occupations. People high on this dimension are an asset to any team. People with high scores on openness to experience enjoy opportunities to reach out to new people and places, while those who are low on this dimension can become stressed or apprehensive in unfamiliar situations. Extroverts like to bounce ideas off other people and to share their worries and concerns. Introverts can also contribute well in team settings but at the end of the day they like their personal reflection time.

Some difficult relationships are in another category altogether. A small proportion of people do not respond well to management, however reasonable. There is the person who will insist on your support for something they want – for example, being given a special project. You explain why this is not possible but the person persists with it and becomes very demanding. Before you know it, they have gone to your boss with a complaint about you. You try to accommodate them in some way. It is not accepted and their behaviour borders on abusive – they are always in the right and you are against them. They go back to your boss, and around and around it goes.

There is no easy answer to managing a person like this. They distort the facts as you see them, expect a lot of your time, and are manipulative. Your best chance of managing them successfully is to work closely with your own boss and have a management plan that you both stick to, one with very clear expectations and boundaries. If you have a team member who fits this pattern, it will be one of your most difficult challenges because they will be a drain on your time and energy; it will stress you and sap the morale of the whole team. Get as much support as you can, and do not blame yourself – some people are almost impossible.

Avoiding leadership derailers

Some people think that how people are treated at work is a peripheral issue – that it doesn't really matter as long as the job gets done. Or that some bosses have unpleasant personalities that we have to put up with. But the fact is, being disrespectful towards others is very damaging. It hurts people, productivity and the leader's credibility. The upside is that we are talking about behaviour, and not immutable personality characteristics. Even leaders with negative behaviour patterns can change if they are motivated to do so.

In this section we will go to the 'dark side' of leadership behaviour, by considering three destructive behavioural styles that commonly occur. We will refer to them as 'the micromanager', 'the risk taker' and 'the bully'. Each of these styles is known to be a serious leadership and career derailer for those who use it.

The micromanager

Some managers are never satisfied with the quality of the team's work and are highly critical. They stand over people, ever watchful for errors or signs that the quality is not up to their standards. They are picky about minor details and may attempt to take over and do it themselves. Needless to say, delegating is not their strong point. It is hard to reason with them by, for example, asking for more responsibility or elbow room. They demand a lot of people and can be very controlling. They may often stay back late at work and will show their displeasure when team members do not do the same. Another tactic is to keep people in the dark about what is happening elsewhere in the organisation, rather than give them the bigger picture or keep them informed of changes. These behaviours are typical of the micromanager.

Here is a typical scenario:

> Before he even took the job as senior project manager, Michael had heard that his new boss was a control freak. He thought he had the patience to handle her. With every new project he made sure that timelines for delivery were set down in writing, he emailed frequent updates, let her know about any changes and always delivered on time.
>
> Despite his track record over two years, she never seemed to let up. She took pride in her efficiency and wanted to know every detail of his office costs, even down to how much paper he used in the printer. He had to inform her in advance of any meetings with clients so that she could approve the agenda beforehand. If the project was due on Friday, she

would be in his office on Wednesday or Thursday making sure it would be completed. It was as if everything he did was suspect until she had checked it off.

People who micromanage often describe themselves as perfectionists with high standards, or as simply wanting the work to be done properly. There is nothing wrong with having high standards but the truth about perfectionists is something different. For whatever reason, they are motivated to avoid mistakes above all else because they fear being judged harshly if they are caught out. Some also procrastinate – another strategy for avoiding errors. Despite their self-assured appearance, leaders like this are overly critical of themselves and are quite insecure. Micromanaging or taking excessive control is their way of reducing the anxiety that they feel.

When leaders micromanage, team members feel pressured, insecure and not trusted to make even routine decisions. It is a serious confidence sapper. People begin to wonder about themselves and their abilities, and believe their manager thinks they are below par. They expect poor ratings at performance appraisal time but may be surprised at their high scores. It leaves them wondering why their boss does not back off and trust them to get on with it. But that is the problem for the micromanager – while they know that their people are competent, they worry a lot and find it difficult to let go of control.

People learn from taking responsibility, making decisions and even making mistakes. Overcontrolling managers rob them of these opportunities and undermine the trust that is vital to building productive team relationships. If you see a little of yourself in the micromanaging style, especially if you describe yourself as a perfectionist, consider talking it through with a coach or counsellor.

The risk taker

Arrogance and overconfidence have long been recognised as a serious flaw in some leaders. Sun Tzu, in *The Art of War*, lists the failings of military commanders as hubris, arrogance, ambition, greed, impulsiveness, unreliability, egocentricity and irresoluteness. These are the characteristics of the risk-taking style where leaders behave as if they are invincible and make serious errors of judgement by ignoring pertinent information, overinflating the chances of success, and dismissing the voices of those urging greater caution.

History is littered with examples of disasters and failed ventures which, in retrospect, were highly risky undertakings. Before the fall, leaders appear decisive, charismatic or even swashbuckling. Some people admire their apparent confidence. But after the event they look more like impulsive attention seekers.

Consider this recent case[32]:

> On 13th January 2012, the cruise ship Costa Concordia hit a rock and capsized off the coast of Italy, with the loss of 32 lives. Despite detailed planning to ensure all aspects of navigational safety, Captain Schettino had ordered an unexpected change of course in notoriously hazardous waters. This was, apparently, a spur of the moment decision by the Captain to sail closer to shore and show off the ship to friends on the nearby island of Giglio, by performing a manoeuvre known as a salute. In the aftermath, Captain Schettino was described as displaying hubris, ego and arrogance – characteristics familiar to those who know him well.

Why do people take risks that are incomprehensible to others? Overconfidence is a known factor. You may be surprised at how often people overestimate the probability of an outcome they desire or assume that they are better acquainted with the facts than they actually are. Most people hesitate before taking action but the combination of confidence and desire leads some people to take excessive risks. But feeling confident does not necessarily mean you are right. It may simply reflect what you want or hope for, or even your determination to succeed. Think about it – you may be absolutely convinced that you will win the job, or the bet, or the race, but it may not happen. In fact, it often doesn't.

Leaders are generally confident people who often push the limits more than other people. Sometimes you do have to take a chance but it is wise to weigh up the risks carefully before taking action. Overconfidence is the result of unjustified optimism or blindness to the pitfalls. The space shuttle *Challenger* explosion, Chernobyl, the 1941 attack on Pearl Harbor, the dotcom bubble and the GFC were unexpected because experts did not read the signs and underestimated the risks. The message for leaders like yourself is to question your assumptions, encourage team members to share their ideas and express misgivings, and not to mistake your enthusiasm and desire to win for a sure thing. A touch of humility and a cautious approach may not be glamorous, but they beat coming back to earth with a thud.

The bully

Just about any kind of bad behaviour you can name has been labelled as workplace bullying – yelling at someone, being overly critical of them in front of others, making belittling remarks, making someone do the difficult or dirty jobs all the time, or excluding certain people from social activities. Bullying is not only instigated by the person's manager. There are many instances of team members bullying the leader, and one person or a group bullying colleagues.

This example of bullying by a colleague was reported to, and investigated by WorkCover NSW[33]:

> *Brian, a project officer, was subjected to bullying by Mark, a co-worker, over a number of months. The behaviour Brian was subjected to included being told his work was not up to scratch, offensive verbal abuse, threats to get him sacked, telling him that he and his family would end up in the gutter and making insulting comments about his relationship with his wife in front of others. The behaviour Brian was subjected to humiliated and intimidated him. He became severely stressed and anxious and was unable to continue working for the organisation due to the bullying.*

When the bullying behaviour is top down, it is often paraded as tough management, letting off steam or results-driven leadership necessary in the corporate jungle. Even the bullies themselves may not see anything untoward in what they do. But, in fact, bullying is an abuse of power, pure and simple. It is not a legitimate way to bring people into line, even if they are underperforming. In many instances bullying constitutes discrimination or harassment, which is illegal in many countries.

Bullying is toxic and its destructive effects can be difficult to name or identify. It creates anxiety and erodes the confidence of those on the receiving end. Some start to think that the bullying is their own fault. It can and does cause psychological and physical illnesses.

Good leaders empower people, they do not crush them. As a leader, you need to monitor your own use of power and make sure that you use it in a positive way. Because bullying also happens among colleagues, you need to ensure that no individual in your team is subject to gossip, teasing, denigration, exclusion or similar behaviours. If the behaviour of colleagues towards an individual is not welcomed by them, then you should put a stop to it.

Over to you

Possessing strong interpersonal skills is an absolute necessity for leaders in contemporary organisations. The social climate is changing – people want and expect a personalised connection with their leaders. They want to be heard and understood. They generally prefer leaders who are warm, approachable and responsive.

You also need strong interpersonal skills to build a high-performing team of people who are fully engaged in their work. This is hard enough in normal times but under pressure it can be very difficult indeed. For instance, when you are feeling stressed, you will almost certainly seem more withdrawn and less approachable. Over time, this could become a pattern unless you work on your resilience and your capacity to stay on top of things.

In this chapter we also described emotionally intelligent behaviour and the way it can be used to manage difficult people and situations. Emotional intelligence is composed of several skills that you can consciously develop. The most critical of these are self-awareness and the ability to control your own feelings and responses. For leaders in our world, behaving in an emotionally intelligent way is as important as analytical thinking and organisational skills.

Chapter 8
Growing as a leader

Leaders are grown, not made.

Peter Drucker

> *In this final chapter ...*
>
> *You will discover many of the things you can do to develop and grow as a leader. These include reflecting on your experience to increase your learning and building your knowledge of workplace behaviour and group dynamics to enable you to inspire your team. The first 30 days in your new leadership role are critical – the chapter concludes with checklists of activities that will embed your leadership during this critical time.*

Choosing to lead

Stepping up to leadership is a conscious choice in contemporary organisations. Many people have the capability and can do it with the right mix of personal motivation, encouragement and experience. It can be a very satisfying aspect of your self-development over a long period of time.

This book was written to help you to establish yourself as a leader. The earlier chapters argued that leadership is about what you do, rather than who you are, what you look like or any special advantages of personality. Some leaders impress with their air of confidence and ease in the way they deal with people. Others seem quieter, or more in the background. These characteristics are far less important than the credibility and influence they have cultivated and their ability to achieve results with and through their team.

If you sometimes doubt your ability, think that you do not look the part or feel that you are an 'imposter', you are not alone. Such doubts are normal. After all, being a leader has its trying moments – the choices are often difficult and the future is uncertain. You are sometimes squeezed between the conflicting expectations of senior management and those of your team, and relationships are not always easy to manage. Hopefully, this book has bolstered your confidence in your capacity to lead and given you the encouragement to keep trying.

How do your view your leadership? You have two options – you can see your new role as just another step in your career, or you can take on the mantle of leadership, making it an integral part of your professional identity. With the first option you would view leadership as just another set of responsibilities that come your way as you progress up the hierarchy. With the second option, you would internalise the role, take on new attitudes and perspectives, and seek to become a leader.

Becoming a leader and feeling comfortable in the role is the more satisfying path. Leaders who feel 'right' extend and use their influence to make things happen. They are open, consultative, caring and supportive. Through their everyday actions they build teams of willing followers whose capacity to deliver is always rising. Their leadership is geared towards making the situation better for all, and not just for themselves.

You want to be a leader in its fullest sense. Even so, as a person new to the role, you may feel far from comfortable and unsure of how you can own the role or start to feel that you really belong. Warren Bennis[34], one of the first modern writers on leadership, understood this problem and suggested that one way forward for leaders was to build their positive self-regard by working to bring out the best in themselves.

A person with positive self-regard is at home in their own skin, realistic about their strengths and limitations, able to stretch themselves or take sensible risks, and comfortable with points of view that are different from their own. To be an inspiring leader, one who empowers and engages others, you really need to be self-affirming. Leaders who constantly doubt or mistrust themselves are in no position to inspire others.

Here are Bennis's three ways of building positive self-regard:

- ✓ Make your strengths effective and your weaknesses irrelevant. The best leaders identify the things they are good at and accentuate them.
- ✓ Challenge yourself. Leaders are like good athletes, they nurture their strengths by setting stretch goals and getting feedback on how they are progressing.
- ✓ Understand the fit between what your organisation requires and what you can contribute. Know how to apply your efforts to get the best outcomes.

Bennis also described becoming a leader as a journey of self-discovery and said that leaders invent themselves. As a process, developing as a leader is both personal and unique. You should not try to become someone else or mimic a leader you have known and admired. So, what are some ideas you can take with you on your own journey of self-discovery as a leader?

- ✓ Understand that growing as a leader is a process of personal transformation.
- ✓ Accept responsibility for your actions and the impact of your behaviour, intended or unintended, on others.
- ✓ Capitalise on opportunities because we learn from experience.
- ✓ Remember that growth comes from reflecting on experience.
- ✓ Seek feedback from others and accept it graciously.
- ✓ Be aware of any negative self-talk that is sapping your confidence.
- ✓ Don't stay around people who are dragging you down or holding you back.

Growing as a leader is also a social process so be aware of the people around you who want you to succeed. These will include family and friends as well as people in your profession and workplace. No one expects you to do it alone so be ready to call on this network of supporters. Your list should include most of the following:

- ✓ a mentor or coach
- ✓ an experienced leader from your profession
- ✓ at least one professional network that holds regular meetings
- ✓ an informal group of peers to share your good and bad moments
- ✓ a trusted friend, to whom you can disclose anything.

Learning from experience

Of all the above advice, the ability to learn from experience is possibly the most critical of all because it enables you to maximise the benefits from everything else you do. To learn from experience you need to do three things:

- ✓ Commit to action.
- ✓ Learn to reflect on what happened.
- ✓ Develop new approaches and solutions.

It might seem obvious but the best learning comes after setting a course and taking the first steps. Many people miss out because they baulk at the starting gates. Stepping away from an opportunity, procrastination, fear of making a mistake, concern about what others will think, and so on, stops them. Learning something new or doing it for the first time usually feels uncomfortable. It is like learning to drive a car – it takes time and patience but after a while driving feels natural.

The ability to reflect on experience is a learned skill. As Peter Drucker[35] noted, growth is always from within. Growth happens when you take action and then reflect on the aspects of your behaviour that worked and the things you need to modify next time. It is a process that works in cycles like this:

- The leader takes action (for example, talks to a team member about poor performance).
- Later, the leader reflects on how it went, what they said and did, what went well and things they could have done better (leader interrupted the team member when they tried to explain why their performance was poor and as a result the team member became passive and compliant. Leader realises the team member was not committed to change but just wanted the interview to end).
- Leader plans to change her approach at the next meeting in two weeks' time (leader decides to ask more open-ended questions, seek more information from the team member and enter into more discussion).
- Leader puts the new plan into action (leader tries out the plan and it produces a better result. She is determined to make this standard practice).

In brief, personal growth results from a continuous cycle where we act, reflect, make some adjustments for next time, try out the new approach, and do more reflection. Without the ability to reflect we are destined to make the same mistakes over and over again. Fortunately, anyone can learn how to reflect through practice. However, to do it really well, we need a degree of self-awareness, a willingness to confront our own shortcomings, and a preparedness to take responsibility for our own behaviour.

The reflection process can get stuck for one reason or another, resulting in little or no personal growth. Revisit the above scenario – this time with a far less satisfactory outcome. The meeting starts the same way with the leader being very directive, the conversation one-way, and the team member shutting down. Afterwards, the leader feels unhappy with how it went and a little angry with the team member for not being more forthcoming. She sees this as evidence that he is resisting her authority and an indication that he does not really want to improve. She is beginning to think that eventually he will have to be managed out of the organisation. The meeting that follows two weeks later is very much like the first one.

The leader in this scenario has not had a good learning experience. She has failed to consider the impact of her own behaviour on the staff member and is therefore not open to other things that she can do to encourage him to open up and discuss the real issues. In short, the quality of her reflection was very poor. The leader appears to lack the necessary self-knowledge and does not understand that her behaviour has triggered a particular kind of response.

Self-knowledge is not necessarily just from within. It also comes from observing what happens to other people and considering how we would behave in a similar situation, or learning from what they have to say about their own experience. This is why mentors can be so important. They have been there before you and can help you shape a way forward.

You can also develop self-knowledge by seeking feedback from other people, including colleagues, clients, trusted friends, coaches and mentors. As noted in Chapter 3, it is hard to be objective about how others see you and everyone has their blind spots. Reflection is more effective when you have realistic feedback about the impact of your own behaviour, so return to that chapter and review the points about how to do this.

To maximise the learning from your experience you also need some alternative behaviours and courses of action to improve on your original approach. In the above scenario, the leader needed to appreciate that asking open-ended questions, not interrupting, and so on, were behaviours that would elicit a better response from the team member. Sometimes people have a light-bulb moment and realise exactly what they did wrong and what they should do next time. At other times they can see what they did was unsuccessful but do not know why, or have little idea about what else they could do to get a better result. No one has all the answers.

Imagine that either leader in the scenario took their problem to a mentor or coach. What might have happened? They would have discussed the situation leading up to the team member's poor performance. This would have given a broader perspective on the people and relationships involved. They would have talked about the team leader's behaviour in the original meeting and considered how this may have caused the team member to shut down. Alternative ways to handle the conversation would have been considered. Perhaps the team leader would have run through some conversation starters with the coach or mentor to get the meeting off to a smooth start. And she would have been prepared with some proven techniques to manage poor performers. In short, her learning would have been accelerated.

Having a sound understanding of human behaviour, team dynamics and how organisations function as systems is important for leaders. The essentials of what you need to know are covered in this book. Apply what you have learned and you will have a solid foundation for your leadership practice. Reminders of the key points on how to build a team of high performers who gain real satisfaction from their work are covered in the following pages.

Inspiring your team

The ability to inspire others has little to do with your personality but everything to do with how you behave every day as you put your guiding principles as a leader into practice. The quality of your leadership is reflected in the attitudes and behaviour of your team. If they willingly collaborate and perform well over a sustained period, then your leadership is working. It may take some time to build to this level, and there are likely to be setbacks along the way, but when it happens your leadership is a key ingredient.

Inspiring leadership is the key to engagement. The word says it all. People who are engaged are emotionally and intellectually invested in their work because they believe in what they do and gain considerable personal satisfaction from it. Their work is an important expression of who they are and the things they care about.

We can identify people who are engaged from their behaviour. But what causes people to feel engaged, and what gets in the way? It is now apparent from research that a range of workplace factors affect engagement. Recent research[36] arranged several of the key factors into three groups and found that they did impact engagement levels. These groupings are shown in the following diagram.

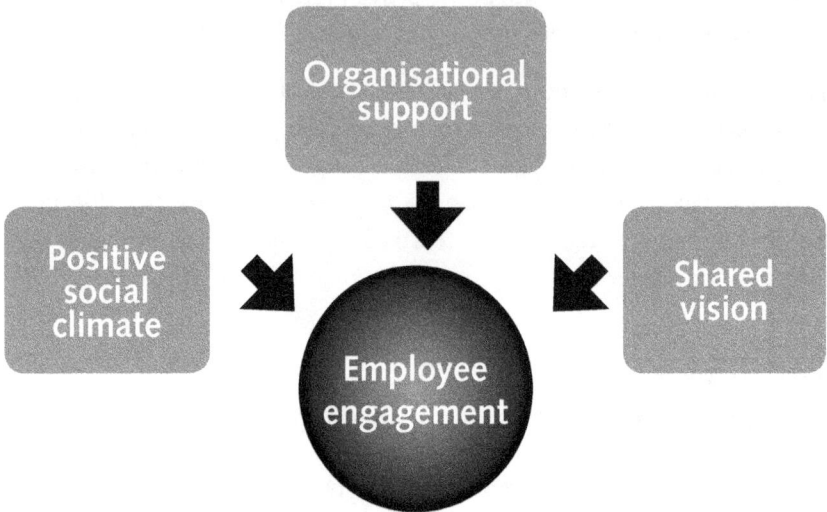

As a leader you set the scene for a **positive social climate**. Fairness, consistency and respect make the workplace feel like a safe place to be. A team culture marked by shared learning and the celebration of milestones and successes creates optimism and a 'can do' attitude.

A positive social climate is more likely when the basic social needs (covered in Chapter 5) are met. It is about responses to the following questions: Am I in or out? Do I have any power and control? And, am I appreciated for what I have to offer? The associated social needs are: belonging (attachment), feeling in control (knowing what is going on and having options), and feeling valued by others. At the extremes we either view ourselves as accepted and included or alienated and on the periphery. We can fully engage only when all three needs are satisfied.

Organisational support means that people believe their organisation cares about their wellbeing and values their contribution. In contemporary workplaces wellbeing is anchored in relationships between leaders and followers that are based on understanding and trust. It is also tied to flexibility where the personal customisation of working conditions allows people to juggle the many demands on their busy lives. People are more likely to engage when their employer focuses more on what they contribute and less on the number of hours they spend on site.

Valuing contributions is a form of organisational support. It is demonstrated in a number of ways, including these:

- ✓ acknowledging achievements
- ✓ linking achievements with individual and group rewards
- ✓ passing on feedback from satisfied customers
- ✓ building on organisational and team strengths
- ✓ providing support and encouragement through the tough times
- ✓ resourcing initiatives that are central to the organisation's mission
- ✓ signalling high expectations of, and confidence in, the capacity of individuals and teams.

The third factor known to affect engagement is **shared vision**. This is important because doing work that is meaningful and based on deeply held values connects to our growth needs. It is even better when those values are part of a vision that we share with others. When we see a real purpose in what we do, we want to do it well, and often strive to achieve personal mastery.

The three factors – positive social climate, organisational support and shared vision – form a complete package. All three need to be in play for high levels of engagement to be sustained over the longer term. Perhaps this helps to explain why only 13% of working people worldwide report that they feel engaged.

Getting the settings right in all three areas is the real test of inspiring leaders. By accepting the mantle of leadership you signal your determination to join their ranks.

In the following story ('Bringing good teamwork to the surface') you will be inspired by what can be achieved when people plan and act together. Sometimes it takes a crisis to show the power of great leadership and teamwork.

Bringing good teamwork to the surface

Most leaders and teams do not know what they are capable of until the unexpected happens. Two incidents involving trapped miners, one in Beaconsfield Tasmania in 2006 and the other in Chile in 2010, captured news headlines around the world while protracted rescue operations were underway. In both cases, due to extraordinary efforts above and below ground, all of the miners were saved.

In Beaconsfield, two miners, Todd Russell and Brant Webb, were wedged in a small cherry picker cage under huge boulders almost a kilometre below the surface. It took six days for mine rescue to detect their location and discover they were still alive. It took another nine days to bring them to the surface. In Chile, 33 miners were trapped for 69 days, 700 metres down. Their whereabouts were not known for 17 days.

The technical challenges facing the rescuers were extremely complex. At Beaconsfield the rock around the cherry picker was unstable, but Russell and Webb kept their nerve and gave vital information as the drilling inched forward through rock five times harder than concrete. Teamwork on the surface was impressive. The planning room worked constantly with options considered, contingencies tested, and people carefully briefed on their roles. While they were 'just ordinary blokes', everyone worked with purpose and professionalism.

The survival of the Chilean miners was due to teamwork and the leadership of their foreman, Luis Urzua. He gathered them in a sheltered area, organised their meagre resources and focused everyone on the essential tasks of survival. Men took on different roles according to their personal strengths. When decisions were needed, everyone had an equal say. Urzua said that this was important for maintaining morale and focusing on common objectives.

These two remarkable examples show what ordinary people can do together when they organise around a common goal, communicate, focus on their strengths, and contribute to finding solutions.

This is a good moment to review the progress that Carl, Margo and Frank have made towards engaging their teams.

Carl genuinely likes people and finds that they take to him quite easily. He has always enjoyed outdoor activities and a wide circle of friends, and has come to see himself as a natural leader. He expected the transition to team leader to be fairly smooth. So he was taken aback by the pockets of resistance and the luke-warm reception to some of his plans and decisions. With the advice of his mentor, Phil, Carl is learning to reflect on his behaviour and now understands why some of his actions were misinterpreted. He is trying to be more transparent and even-handed and has begun to build a cohesive team. He is learning to listen, provide feedback on performance and do more to reward and motivate people.

Margo, like many other professionals, works in an organisation where leadership training is an afterthought, if it is provided at all. She was promoted to the team leader position because of her excellent discipline-based qualifications and professionalism. When she arrived she could see that the team was capable and committed and decided to put her energies into organising the admin and casework files. In doing so, she drifted towards the liberal style of the laissez-faire leader. Early on though, the morale problem caught her attention and made her think. She now realises that the physiotherapists need her support so is using the new patient management software to free up time and spend it with them. There will be more consultation and everyone will share in making decisions about patient management and other important issues. As her leadership evolves, Margo will create an environment where people have more scope to satisfy their growth needs, including the satisfaction of appreciating that what they do together is genuinely worthwhile.

Frank had a rather shaky start in his role as a team leader in the suburban supermarket. He faced covert resistance – people did what he wanted them to do only when he was watching. His controlling style of leadership was the problem. To his great credit, Frank was willing to change. He has stopped blaming individuals and has started to build relationships. He is working with the team to optimise workflows from the delivery trucks to the supermarket shelves and to improve food handling standards. Trust and cohesion are starting to build. Ultimately, Frank and the team will see the benefits in happier customers, and their personal satisfaction from working in that environment will rise also.

Carl, Margo and Frank are not there yet, but all have made an excellent start. For them it was a matter of meeting the team, assessing the situation and learning how to take people along with them. In the final sections of this chapter we will cover some key ideas and actions that will help you to establish your leadership in the early stages.

The first 30 days

From the first day onwards, behave like the kind of leader who is intent on building a team of willing followers who are engaged and productive. Do not feel that you have to assert your authority, be accepted immediately or have all the answers. Influence, acceptance and know-how will come in time as you develop your empowering leadership style. Some of the tactics that will help you build in the early days and weeks include these:

- ✓ Move away from your desk and build relationships.
- ✓ Clarify your role and responsibilities with your manager.
- ✓ Be interested in what people are doing.
- ✓ Ask questions and listen to the answers.
- ✓ Always get all sides of the story before forming an opinion.
- ✓ Notice how the culture works – 'the way we do things around here'.
- ✓ Get a feel for the social climate and where the energy resides.

Effective leaders build their knowledge and capabilities in relation to three domains that are covered extensively in this book. Here is a reminder of what they are, followed by some ideas about what you might prioritise during your first 30 days in your new role.

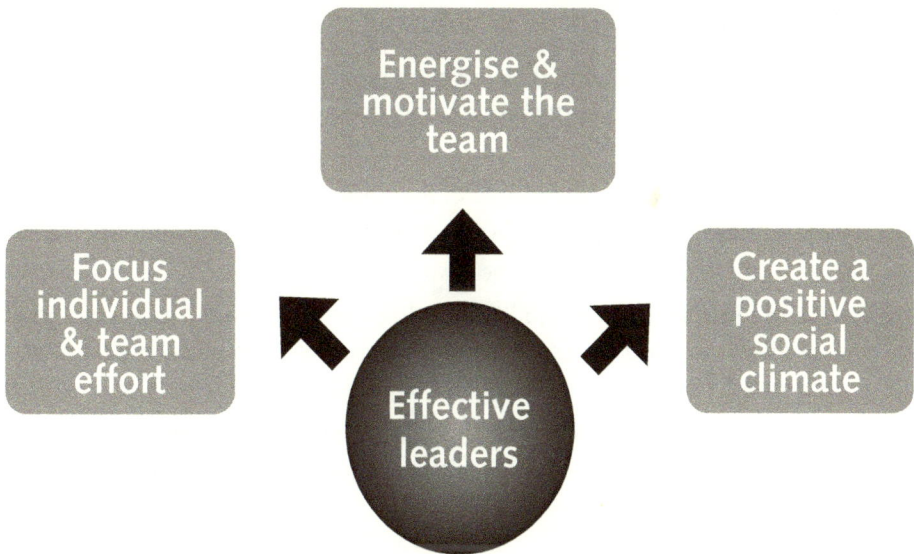

Focus individual and team effort

When you step up to the leadership role, you need to take what is sometimes called a helicopter view of things. Before, you were absorbed in your own projects, but now you see things from above, noting who is accountable for what, how smoothly the work is flowing, and what is happening in the larger organisation.

Focusing individual and team effort means:

- making sure that individual roles and responsibilities are clear and unambiguous and never assuming that people have the same understanding of the priorities and standards of work or service that you, yourself, have.
- keeping the work flowing smoothly in and around the team.
- aligning the day-to-day activities of the team with business objectives.
- knowing about the strategic priorities of your organisation and what or how your team contributes.

So in the early days you might do the following:

- ✓ Meet with every individual to review their roles, responsibilities, matters that they consider to be priorities, and any unresolved issues relating to their work.

- ✓ Check where every individual is in the performance review cycle, and where they stand in terms of their professional development and career planning.

- ✓ Use the **role and responsibility charting tool** (Chapter 5) to assess how work flows around the team, noting where there are gaps, overlaps or bottlenecks.

- ✓ Collect and review information and data from a variety of sources about the team's performance levels and progress towards business objectives.

Meetings with individuals should be consultative – let them understand that you are interested in them and their work and are not seeking to find fault. In relation to workflows and the whole team, the role and responsibility charting tool can be used by yourself in a desk exercise or as a discussion starter for team meetings. Using a tool like this centres attention on the productivity issues rather than personalities – very useful when there is some inefficiency or confusion and this is causing conflict.

A key point to remember in any joint problem-solving discussions is that you are seeking to:

- ✓ bring people closer together so that they can work on the issues, and

- ✓ avoid any process that polarises opinions and drives people apart.

A safe way to do this is to draw attention to what is working well and the strengths of the team, before moving on to things that could be done more efficiently, for example, or what might improve the customer experience. Staying positive raises the energy level in the room, while pointing out people's deficiencies brings it down. When the energy is high people are more positive, creative and capable of generating solutions.

Energise and motivate the team

The extent to which your team is energised and motivated depends on several factors associated with your leadership and the broader organisation. You do not control everything that is relevant but you are not without options either. Your best approach is to develop a sound reward strategy to motivate your team to perform at its best. It will work if you do this in tandem with developing the other two knowledge and capability domains (focusing effort and creating a positive social climate).

Rewarding people for their efforts and results helps them to perform to their potential. It reinforces the behaviours that lead to the outcomes you want, and motivates people to continue building their skills and capability. A good reward strategy provides opportunities to satisfy our existence, relatedness and growth needs. These needs are met in different ways, so you need several components in your reward strategy.

The three planks of your reward strategy were covered in Chapter 6.

- Use your organisation's extrinsic rewards to acknowledge good work. Your words of thanks, praise and advice are just as important. Indeed, it is almost impossible to be too liberal in acknowledging people who are helping you to make a difference or working towards a great outcome. Very few people complain that they receive too much feedback.
- Ensure that every job in your team is intrinsically rewarding. This happens when interest, challenge and an appropriate degree of autonomy are built in. Jobs that are intrinsically rewarding satisfy some of our growth needs, and these are associated with engagement and high-quality work.
- Link work with core values. Foster team values by giving the mission and vision of your organisation meaning through the things that your team strives to accomplish together. Encourage employees to live up to the standards and values of their profession.

During the first 30 days in your new role, do the following as you begin to plan your reward and motivation strategy:

✓ Review the policies of your organisation as they relate to salary rises, other financial inducements, promotions, development opportunities, special leave entitlements (like study leave), flexible working arrangements and other provisions to encourage or reward employees.

✓ Enquire about how the above are implemented (for example, used liberally or not at all), how aware the team members are about their availability, how willing they are to ask for access to them, and perceptions about the fairness or otherwise in their allocation.

✓ Use the **Job Characteristics Model** and related materials (Chapter 6) to assess the motivational potential of the jobs held by team members.

✓ Notice how aware team members are about the mission, vision and values of your organisation, and the extent to which they bring them to life through their work. Also take note of team strengths, achievements that give them the most satisfaction and stories about the best or most difficult moments from the past.

✓ Consult with highly qualified professionals (if members of your team) to gauge how they feel about the level of organisational support they receive and especially any factors that inhibit their capacity to do their best work.

As before, use a consultative approach in any meetings you have with individuals and the team as a whole. Be interested and encourage people to open up. You will also learn much by simply standing back and observing how people behave in general, the stories they tell and the experiences they relate.

Note that there is often a disconnect between the extrinsic rewards provided for in the policies and procedures manuals, and their implementation. Sometimes people do not know what is available to them, or they are subtly discouraged from asking or applying. For example, a person may be concerned that taking study leave will be interpreted as a lack of commitment to the current job and worry that this could lead to repercussions from their manager. So be alert to any circumstances like this.

Towards the end of your first 30 days in the leadership role, you should have enough information and insights to start forming your strategy. Make sure that you have one or two firm ideas to implement from each of the three planks.

Create a positive social climate

A positive social climate is an essential ingredient for enabling sustainable, high performance. The workplace should feel welcoming, safe and supportive, thus satisfying some of the existence needs. This is a necessary foundation for all of the other things you do to encourage people to do their best work. If the workplace climate lacks these features, you are likely to be frustrated in your efforts to generate energy, creativity or collaboration.

A positive social climate also supports the satisfaction of many of our relatedness needs. People are social beings above all else. We seek the support of other people and we are sensitive to their thoughts and feelings. For most people, activities and achievements are better when they are shared, and much of our self-esteem is moulded by the acceptance and regard we receive from others. A positive social climate is therefore critical for teamwork and shared learning.

You can promote a positive social climate in the following ways:

- Ensure that the basic conditions – physical and psychological – are conducive to positive interactions among team members and that negative influences, such as criticism, bullying and being ignored, are removed.
- Ensure that the workplace is conducive to satisfying relatedness needs and that factors in the workplace support the development of self-esteem and feelings of shared accomplishment.
- Humanise the workplace by being the kind of leader who is approachable, fair, consistent and genuinely interested in each individual's welfare, interests, hopes and aspirations.

Use your first 30 days as leader to assess and begin to mould the social climate by doing the following:

- ✓ Learn relevant facts about the team's past history (for example, redundancies, performance problems or upsets of any kind) from your manager.

- ✓ Assess the physical workplace conditions for factors such as noise, space (crowding is detrimental to relationships), furnishings and recreational spaces.

- ✓ Observe the everyday interactions of team members (face to face, in meetings and through social media) and note the extent to which civility and respect are the norm.

- ✓ Use the **team dynamics checklist** (Chapter 5) to assess the extent to which every person feels included, in control, and valued for what they have to offer.

- ✓ Model the standards of behaviour you expect everyone to meet.

- ✓ Begin the process of forming a supportive relationship with every person in your team, show a genuine interest, and always follow up on commitments you make to them.

Getting a feel for the team's social dynamics will take some time, and you might uncover some sticking points or unresolved issues. Ask your manager to fill you in on such things. There may have been staff losses, formal complaints, or any number of other problems in the past, so size these up quickly and help the team to move on. If there are serious unresolved problems bugging the team, these are likely to show up as absenteeism or other performance issues.

Sometimes apparently simple things like the physical work environment affect relationships and small adjustments can make all the difference, so identify any factor disrupting the smooth flow of communication and try to remedy it. If people are not very happy or comfortable, this may show up in the way they relate, so notice if standards of civility and respect meet your expectations of what they should be.

With these fundamentals in hand, you can shift your attention towards the psychological factors, especially the extent to which people's basic social needs are met. You can use the **team dynamics checklist** (Chapter 5) as a general guide for your enquiries as you form relationships with individual team members. Considering their feelings and experiences through this lens should give you some useful ideas about where to start building.

Most of all, from the first day, be a role model for the way that you want people in your team to interact with one another. Regardless of whether the quality of relationships is already good or less than it should be, show through your example what you expect of everyone into the future.

Over to you

You have reached the end of this book but hopefully are just at the beginning of a new stage in your growth as a leader.

In these pages you have a complete guide for managing people and teams. You now know that effective leaders build their knowledge and capabilities in relation to three domains of leadership practice – focusing on outcomes, energising and motivating the team, and building a positive social climate. Use these ideas in the ways suggested and you will develop the capability to inspire others to produce excellent results and gain real satisfaction from their work.

Growing as a leader is a lifelong endeavour. If you are like most others, you will start out feeling a little unsure of yourself, but with experience your confidence will grow. Reflecting on experience and building positive self-regard are essential, but you will also learn from mentors who have been there before you, coaches who will help to accelerate your learning, and others in your support team who want you to succeed.

For more inspiration and great ideas,
go to the author website
and sign up for the regular newsletter:

www.drjudithchapman.com

Endnotes

1. When it comes to gaining insights into leadership, there are few better reads than *The Art of War*. The various surviving fragments of this work were written during the Era of the Warring States in Ancient China. Due to the extraordinary insights of the military strategists who wrote it (Sun Tzu and others) and the many metaphors for leadership in civil society that it contains, the text has been very influential in modern business teaching: Sun Tzu II (translated by Thomas Cleary, 1966), *The Art of War*. HarperSanFrancisco.

2. Field Marshal Sir William Slim fought in the two World Wars, most notably at Gallipoli and in the Burma campaign. He was an effective leader who lifted morale and was highly regarded by the troops. In 1953 he was appointed Governor-General of Australia. These words are from a speech he made to the Australian Institute of Management in Adelaide on 4 April 1957.

3. The idea of followership was introduced by Robert Kelley as the reciprocal social process of leadership. He gave the main qualities of effective followers as the ability to self-manage, commitment, competence and the capacity to hold true to their beliefs and ethical standards: Kelley, R. E. (1988), In praise of followers. *Harvard Business Review*, 66, 142-148.

4. Covey, S. R. (1989), *The 7 Habits of Highly Effective People*. The Business Library, N.Y.

5. Stories about Gail Kelly have appeared in many publications. Those used for this profile include *Boss* (11 & 12 Sep 2014) and *The Age* (3 July 2005).

6. Legal-rational authority is bureaucratic, meaning that the authority comes from institutional rules that are outside the control of those who must administer them. The term was introduced by the sociologist Max Weber in a 1922 essay, and his influential ideas were translated from German into English in 1958.

7. Clayton Alderfer's ERG theory (1969) was a condensation of Maslow's Hierarchy of Needs that has five need categories.

8. Cutting-edge research in neuroscience has demonstrated that our attitudes and behaviours are linked to brain patterns that leaders can influence. By behaving in certain ways leaders can enhance the social climate and create the conditions for wellbeing and productivity. The theory and practice of neuroscience as it applies to leadership is explained in this wonderful book: Henson, C. & Rossouw, P. (2013), *Brain Wise Leadership: Practical Neuroscience to Survive and Thrive at Work*. Learning Quest, Sydney.

9. Warren Bennis wrote and lectured extensively on the subject of leadership and is widely regarded as a pioneer in this field. The ideas here are from this book: Bennis, W. & Townsend, R. (1995), *Reinventing Leadership: Strategies to Empower the Organisation*. Quill, N.Y.

10. Copyright © (2014) Gallup, Inc. All rights reserved. The content is used with permission; however, Gallup retains all rights of publication.

11. Rosabeth Moss Kanter is a professor of business at Harvard University and is a highly respected author of many books and articles on leadership and organisational change. She discussed the use of power and the benefits of empowering employees in this book: Kanter, R.M. (1977), *Men and Women of the Corporation*. Basic Books, N.Y.

12. Lewin, K., Lippit, R. & White, R. (1939), Patterns of aggressive behavior in experimentally created social climates. *Journal of Social Psychology*, 10, 271-301.

13. Details about these war-time experiments can be found in Kurt Lewin's biography: Marrow, A.J. (1969), *The Practical Theorist*. Basic Books, N.Y.

14. A collection of Mary Parker Follett's essays are available in this publication: Graham, P. (2003), *Mary Parker Follett, Prophet of Management: A Celebration of Writings from the 1920s*. Beard Books, District of Columbia.

15. Elton Mayo was an Australian who studied at Adelaide University and was later appointed to Harvard Business School. He was a critic of the Scientific Management approach and emphasised the importance of social relationships at work. He was one of the founders of the discipline of Organisational Behaviour.

16. McGregor, D. (1960), *The Human Side of Enterprise*. McGraw-Hill, N.Y.

17. Robert Rosenthal did many experiments to show that labelling can affect behaviour (e.g. referring to people as unreliable, black, stupid, or any other term that might elicit prejudices). This experiment was reported in: Rosenthal, R. & Fode, K. (1963). The effect of experimenter bias on performance of the albino rat. *Behavioral Science*, 8, 183-189.

18. Rosenthal, R. & Jacobson, L. (1968), *Pygmalion in the Classroom*. Holt, Rinehart & Winston, N.Y.

19. Frederick Taylor's ideas were highly influential during the time of significant industrial development and turbulence from the 1880s until the 1920s.

20. This story is based on Adam Smith's pin factory, in which he illustrated and recommended the productivity advantages of a high division of labour in industry. His ideas are found in his famous book, *Wealth of Nations*, published in 1776.

21. This is discussed in this classic resource on organisational behaviour: Weisbord, M.R. (2004), *Productive Workplaces Revisited: Dignity, Meaning and Community in the 21ˢᵗ Century*. Jossey-Bass, San Francisco.

22. Epstein, S. (1990), Cognitive-experiential self-theory. In Pervin, L.A. (ed.), *Handbook of Personality: Theory and Research* (pp.165-192). Guildford Press, N.Y.

23. Grawe, K. (2007), *Neuropsychotherapy: How the Neurosciences Inform Effective Psychotherapy*. Lawrence Erlbaum Associates Publishers, Mahwah NJ.

24. Jack Welch is a former chair and CEO of General Electric. During his 20 years leading that company its wealth increased immeasurably. Not surprisingly, his ideas on corporate strategy are highly regarded. Welch was drawing on the insights of the Prussian general

Von Clausewitz when he said, 'strategy is the evolution of a central idea through continually changing circumstances' (*The Economist*, 7 March 2002).

25. Brosnan, S.F. & de Waal, F.B.M. Monkeys reject unequal pay. *Nature*, 425, pp.297-299, 18 Sept 2003.

26. William Edwards Deming was an American engineer who developed techniques to improve production processes, known as 'total quality management (TQM)'. His ideas were initially taken up by Japanese industry and led to a significant turnaround in quality of production and economic prosperity. TQM was later adopted in many industrialised countries. At the core of his approach were 14 principles, in which technical innovations were combined with an empowering style of management. The principles were widely publicised through his book *Out of the Crisis* (1986). MIT Press, Cambridge, MA.

27. The Job Characteristics Model was originally presented by Greg Oldham and Richard Hackman, although it is based on the earlier contributions of many others. The central idea was that enriched jobs (those containing the core job characteristics) increased the job holder's sense that they had real responsibility, that their work was meaningful, and that they understood its impact on clients and other stakeholders. As a result of this they felt motivated to perform and their job satisfaction increased. That is why we can say that enriched jobs have greater motivational potential than simplified jobs. The model has been extensively researched and discussed in the management literature.

28. Fred Emery was an Australian psychologist and a leading exponent of employee participation in decision making, job redesign/enrichment, and self-managing teams. His field work in the UK and Norway with Eric Trist and others in the 1950s and 1960s led to important advances in our understanding of organisational and human systems (based on a framework known as 'open systems theory'). With his wife, Merrelyn Emery, he developed participative planning processes that are still influential today. The list of job characteristics here is one that Fred, himself, used (similar to, but not the same as the original Oldham and Hackman list).

29. Job Diagnostic Survey, developed by Richard Hackman and Greg Oldham.

30. Drucker, P. (1954), *The Practice of Management*. Harper, N.Y. His quote 'you cannot hire a hand ...' can be found on page 262.

31. Daniel Goleman has written several interesting books on the topic of emotional intelligence. If you would like to learn more about this topic – the research studies and what others have to say on the topic – visit this website: Consortium for Research on Emotional Intelligence in Organizations.

32. This accident was extensively covered by the world's news services. The story here is constructed from a number of these sources.

33. WorkCover NSW. Preventing and responding to bullying at work. http://www.workcover.nsw.gov.au/formspublications/publications/Documents/bullying_at_work_2054.pdf. Accessed 26 Oct 2014.

34. Bennis, W. & Townsend, R. (1995), *Reinventing Leadership: Strategies to Empower the Organisation*, Quill, N.Y., pp. 30-31.

35. Drucker, P. (1954), *The Practice of Management*. Harper, N.Y. p.266.

36. Mahon, E.G., Taylor, S.N. & Boyatzis, R.E., Antecedents of organizational engagement: exploring vision, mood and perceived organizational support with emotional intelligence as a moderator. *Frontiers in Psychology*, 18 Nov 2014.

www.ingramcontent.com/pod-product-compliance
Lightning Source LLC
Chambersburg PA
CBHW031124020426
42333CB00012B/225